ESSENTIAL
COSTA DEL SOL

★ Best places to see 34–55

■ Featured sight

Málaga 83–101

West of Málaga 102–166

East of Málaga 167–186

Original text by Mona King

Updated by Mary Laurie

© Automobile Association Developments Limited 2009

First published 2007

Reprinted 2009. Information verified and updated

ISBN: 978-0-7495-6006-5

Published by AA Publishing, a trading name of Automobile Association Developments
Limited, whose registered office is Fanum House, Basing View, Basingstoke,
Hampshire RG21 4EA. Registered number 1878835.

Colour separation: MRM Graphics Ltd

Printed and bound in Italy by Printer Trento S.r.l.

A03616

Maps in this title produced from mapping:

© ISTITUTO GEOGRAFICO DE AGOSTINI, Novara - 2008

© Freytag-Berndt u. Artaria KG, 1231 Vienna-Austria

About this book

This book is divided into five sections.

The essence of the Costa del Sol
pages 6–19
Introduction; Features; Food and drink; Short break including the 10 Essentials

Planning pages 20–33
Before you go; Getting there; Getting around; Being there

Best places to see pages 34–55
The unmissable highlights of any visit to the Costa del Sol

Best things to do pages 56–79
Good places to have lunch; activities; beaches; places to take the children; stunning views and more

Exploring pages 80–186
The best places to visit in the Costa del Sol, organized by area

Maps
All map references are to the maps on the covers. For example, Málaga has the reference ✚ 20K – indicating the grid square in which it is to be found

Admission prices
€ inexpensive (under €3)
€€ moderate (€3–€6)
€€€ expensive (over €6)

Hotel prices
Price are per room per night:
€ budget (under €65);
€€ moderate (€65–€150);
€€€ expensive to luxury (over €150)

Restaurant prices
Price for a three-course meal per person without drinks:
€ budget (under €20);
€€ moderate (€20–€40);
€€€ expensive (over €40)

Contents

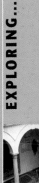

The essence of. . .

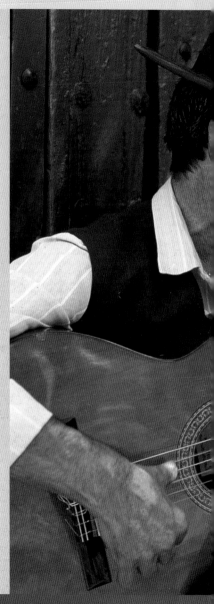

The Costa del Sol is all about year-round fun and sun.
The essential ingredients are here: sandy beaches,
sunshine, great hotels and restaurants, plus bars,
entertainment and sporting pursuits, from a leisurely
round of golf to a vigorous course in kitesurfing. Away
from the coast, the countryside is stunning, while the
Costa capital of Málaga has big-city sophistication,
with museums, theatres and stylish shops.

features

For many, mention of the Costa del Sol conjures up visions of suntanned bodies on the beach, luxurious hotels set in tropical gardens, golfing and glitzy marinas lined with millionaires' yachts, lively restaurants and sophisticated clubs – in other words, the high life, where you might rub shoulders with celebrities. Since its popularity took off in the 1960s and it became the 'in place' for the jet set, it has had its ups and downs, but it has regained its position as a top year-round destination.

The atmosphere is cosmopolitan, and many expatriates have settled here with a particularly high concentration around Torremolinos, Marbella and Fuengirola. Between 2008 and 2013 at least 200,000 families from other parts of Europe are expected to buy homes in Málaga province, adding to the 65,000 foreigners already living here.

Although times have changed, the Costa del Sol still has great appeal. The tendency is now to seek more seclusion, however, with much of the entertaining and partying taking place in private. But the Costa del Sol still exudes an aura of glamour, which serves as a magnet to visitors. Its mild, sunny winter climate, unrivalled in Europe, is an additional attraction.

More recently, there has been an effort to encourage visitors to look beyond the beach-only holiday, and to sample the more rural pleasures of the hinterland. The Costa del Sol is an excellent gateway to the beautiful interior of Andalucía with its enchanting white towns and villages, peaceful landscapes and its real jewels, the historic cities of Córdoba and Granada, and Sevilla – all of which can easily be reached by bus or train or by taking a tour. Local travel agencies or your hotel can help.

thicker version of *gazpacho* and *ajo blanco*, based on crushed garlic and almonds, served with grapes. *Sopa de rape* is among the many excellent fish soups you can find.

Fritura malagueña – an assortment of fried fish – is typical of coastal cooking. Other dishes to look out for are cod *à la Málaga*, fish chowders, casserole of dogfish, cockles, crayfish and prawns grilled or served *al pil-pil* (sizzling with garlic and chilli). Roasted sardines and fresh anchovies can also be delicious and rice dishes such as a *risotto à la marinera* (seafood) or *paella* are usually a good bet.

Empanadas (pies with a tuna filling) and *pimientos à la malaguena* (peppers Málaga-style) are other local dishes to sample. *Puchero* is a sort of country casserole with chickpeas.

Up in the hills above Málaga you can come

across tasty varieties of sausages from the different regions. Try the *morcillas* of Antequera, *embutidos* from Ronda and *chorizo* produced in Benaofán. *Conejo* (rabbit) or *pollo al ajillo* (chicken with garlic) are popular dishes and kid is also a delicacy here. The Alpujarras is famous for its hams and produces pork dishes, such as suckling pig.

Worth a mention among the desserts are *yemas del tajo*, based on egg yolks and sugar, *dulce de membrillo*, made from quinces and there is always the ubiquitous *flan* (crème caramel). A typical way to round off a meal, however, is with the fresh fruit of the season.

Chiringuitos is the name given to beach bars and restaurants. They are to be found all along the coast, ranging from simple open-air huts, with a casual atmosphere, to more sophisticated eateries. These are often very good places to sample traditional Spanish dishes, with an emphasis on fresh fish and seafood, either fried or grilled and served with a simple salad.

WINE

Málaga is known for its wines. Although there are dry varieties it is famous primarily for its sweet wines, produced from the grapes of La Axarquía.

Some excellent sweet dessert wines are grown in the vineyards around Cómpeta where it is possible to try wine-tasting. Farther inland, some very acceptable wines are produced in the Montilla-Moriles area. Although not a local product, a jug of *sangría* (red wine, fruit and lemonade), served chilled with ice, is a pleasant accompaniment to a meal on a warm day. A popular liqueur is *aguardiente de Ojén*.

short break

Even if you have only a short time to visit the Costa del Sol it's still possible to get a real taste of the area and create some unforgettable memories along the way. The following suggestions will give you a wide range of sights and experiences that won't take very long, won't cost very much and will make your visit special.

● **Do the daytime scene** in Puerto Banús, the place to hang out. Linger over a drink at the Sinatra Bar (► 55) or the Saladuba Pub (► 55) on the waterfront and admire the luxurious yachts moored in the marina – you might even spot a celebrity or two. Then move on for a long lunch at one of the stylish open-air restaurants on the quayside. When you've had your fill relax on the lovely sandy beach discreetly tucked away at one end of the port.

● **Eat *tapas*** in a local bar. *Tapas* bars are a way of life in Spain and a visit to some of these establishments will give you a feel of the place. A lively atmosphere is usually provided by the locals, who meet regularly for animated

conversation over a beer or a chilled *fino* sherry. The choice of *tapas* can range from olives, almonds, *jamón serrano* (cured ham), to *tortilla* slices (Spanish-style omelettes), vegetable dishes and a selection of fish and seafood dishes, often well laced with garlic. *Porciones* denote smaller helpings, while *raciones* are more ample. The bars are open for most of the day to serve drinks and food.

● **Wander around** Málaga's historic city centre with its majestic, unfinished Gothic cathedral, surrounded by ochre buildings and narrow pedestrian streets; the latter lined with tapas bars and intriguing shops. Don't miss the Alcazaba (➤ 36–37) and the views from the castle.

● **Check to see whether there is a local festival** in the area you are visiting. If there is, make sure you attend and be ready to party. With their colour and exuberance they are celebrations of life itself. Many are religious events; there are pilgrimages, celebrations for patron saints, fairs and festivals connected with fishermen and the sea. Flamenco fairs and bullfight festivals, concerts and numerous cultural events add to the list.

● **Walk up to the Alcazaba and Gibralfaro** for the panoramic views over Málaga and the bay. Málaga's Alcazaba (➤ 36–37) has a wonderful sense of antiquity in its rough walls and in the maze of terraces, gardens, patios and cobbled ramps that lead ever upwards through impressive archways into the sunlight.

- **See an authentic flamenco show** where its roots belong. For the visitor who wishes to experience something 'typically Spanish', there are plenty of nightspots along the Costa with flamenco shows which can be colourful and entertaining. The true magic of flamenco, however, is spontaneity and real passion, which is not so easy to find. You could experience some good flamenco at a local fiesta, or tucked away in the back streets of towns such as Sevilla or Málaga accompanied, ideally, by someone who knows where to look.

- **Have an early evening drink** on Marbella's Paseo Marítimo (➤ 120) and watch the sunset, taking in a wide view of the Rock of Gibraltar and coastline of Africa. Then take a stroll along the promenade until you find a suitable restaurant where you can linger over a meal.

- **Do the rounds of Banús by night**. After dark the Puerto Banús takes on a totally different perspective; when the sun goes down things start to hot up and the glitterati come out to play. The action starts around midnight and continues until dawn with dozens of discos, bars and clubs. You can try your luck at the casino but be careful as the stakes are high here.

- **Drive up into the hills** to visit one of the many *pueblos blancos*, the 'white towns', and hilltop villages, and enjoy the magnificent views. Mijas, Casares, Gaucín and Frigiliana are fine examples of these delightful mountain retreats.

- **Visit Ronda** to admire its stunning setting and famous old bridge. The Puente Nuevo hangs like a wedge over a deep gorge, and is the subject of countless paintings and photographs. The views down across the ravine are spectacular, and the town itself is unspoiled and attractive.

Planning

Before you go

WHEN TO GO

JAN	FEB	MAR	APR	MAY	JUN	JUL	AUG	SEP	OCT	NOV	DEC
16°C	17°C	18°C	21°C	23°C	27°C	29°C	29°C	27°C	23°C	19°C	17°C
61°F	63°F	64°F	70°F	73°F	81°F	84°F	84°F	81°F	73°F	66°F	63°F

● High season　○ Low season

Temperatures are the **average daily maximum** for each month. Easter is usually bright and sunny without being too hot; however, accommodation is heavily booked up. The best time to visit is in May and early June when there is plenty of sunshine and the average daytime temperature is 23°C (73°F) to 25°C (77°F). Visitor levels are not too high and there is a choice of where to stay. Peak tourist times are in July and August, when the weather is hottest. Most of the country is on holiday in August and there is a huge exodus to the coast. September and October can be delightful with sunny weather lingering well into autumn. Winters on the coast and in low-lying regions are pleasant, but in the mountains expect chilly weather.

WHAT YOU NEED

● Required
○ Suggested
▲ Not required

Some countries require a passport to remain valid for a minimum period (usually at least six months) beyond the date of entry – contact their consulate or embassy or your travel agent for details.

	UK	Germany	USA	Netherlands
Passport (or National Identity Card where applicable)	●	●	●	●
Visa (regulations can change – check before you travel)	▲	▲	▲	▲
Onward or Return Ticket	▲	▲	●	▲
Health Inoculations (tetanus and polio)	▲	▲	▲	▲
Health Documentation (➤ 23, Health Advice)	●	●	●	●
Travel Insurance	○	○	○	○
Driving Licence (national)	●	●	●	●
Car Insurance Certificate	●	●	●	●
Car Registration Document	●	●	●	●

WEBSITES

www.andalucia.org
www.gospain.org
www.andalucia.com

www.malagaturismo.com
www.visitcostadelsol.com

TOURIST OFFICES AT HOME

In the UK

Spanish Tourist Office,
22/23 Manchester Square, London
W1M 5AP ☎ (020) 7486 8077;
www.uk.tourspain.es

In the USA

Tourist Office of Spain,
666 Fifth Avenue 35th,
New York, NY 10103
☎ (212) 265 8822;
www.okspain.org

Tourist Office of Spain,
8383 Wilshire Boulevard, Suite 960,
Beverley Hills, CA 90211
☎ (323) 658 7188;
www.okspain.org

HEALTH ADVICE

Insurance Nationals of EU countries are entitled to some free medical treatment in Spain with the relevant documentation (form EHIC for Britons) although private medical insurance is still advised and is essential for all other visitors.

Dental services Dental treatment normally has to be paid for in full as dentists operate privately. A list of dentists can be found in the yellow pages of the telephone directory. Dental treatment should be covered by private medical insurance.

TIME DIFFERENCES

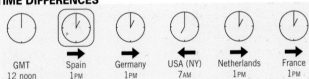

GMT	Spain	Germany	USA (NY)	Netherlands	France
12 noon	1PM	1PM	7AM	1PM	1PM

Spain is one hour ahead of Greenwich Mean Time (GMT+1), but from late March until the Saturday before the last Sunday in October, summer time (GMT+2) operates.

PLANNING

NATIONAL HOLIDAYS

1 Jan *New Year's Day*

6 Jan *Epiphany*

28 Feb *Andalusian Day (regional)*

Mar/Apr *Maundy Thursday, Good Friday, Easter Monday*

1 May *Labour Day*

24 Jun *San Juan (regional)*

25 Jul *Santiago (regional)*

15 Aug *Assumption of the Virgin*

12 Oct *National Day*

1 Nov *All Saints' Day*

6 Dec *Constitution Day*

8 Dec *Feast of the Immaculate Conception*

25 Dec *Christmas Day*

Most shops, offices and museums close on these days.

WHAT'S ON WHEN

January *Los Reyes Magos* (6 January). In Málaga and all major coastal resorts the Three Kings throw sweets from grand floats.

February/March *Carnaval* (the week before Lent) in Málaga, Granada and Antequera. Floats, colourful costumes, music and dancing.

March/April *Semana Santa* (Holy Week, moveable date) in Sevilla, Málaga and Granada. From Palm Sunday to Easter Sunday there are nightly processions of *cofradías* (brotherhoods) carrying images of the saints or the Virgin; wearing pointed hoods, each carries a lighted candle. The muffled drums are accompanied by the occasional *saeta* (improvised religious lament).

April *Fería de Sevilla* (Seville Fair). Originally a cattle fair, the *fería* has evolved into a world-famous event of colour, music and *flamenco*. The daily horseback parade is a special attraction with the men in dashing outfits and their ladies decked out in traditional flamboyant dresses. Every afternoon bullfights take place in the Maestranza ring with the most famous of Spain's matadors.

May *Las Cruces de Mayo* (early May). This represents an ancient custom when crosses decorated with both real and paper flowers are placed in the streets and squares. The fiesta is particularly attractive in Torrox and Coín.

May/June *Corpus Christi* (moveable date). Processions pass along flower-strewn streets. They are especially colourful in Granada, with parades, music and dancing.

July *La Virgen del Carmen* (16 July). The most spectacular events are at Los Boliches, Fuengirola; also at Torremolinos, Marbella and Nerja. The patron saint of fishermen is paraded through the streets before being taken around the bay on a boat; fireworks, music and dancing on the beach.

September *Pedro Romero Fiestas* (early September). Ronda celebrates the bullfighter with *corridas Goyescas* (Goya-style bullfights), with top matadors in costume from Goya's time.

October *Feria del Rosario*. This fair is celebrated in Fuengirola during the first two weeks in October. *Casetas* (clubhouses) of various societies and brotherhoods set up between Fuengirola and Los Boliches offer shows, food and drink. A lively affair, with horseback-riding events, flamenco and fireworks.

December *Fiesta de Verdiales* (29 December). In La Venta de San Cayetano, in Puerto de la Torre, Málaga. Colourfully attired *pandas* (musical groups) compete with each other; a lively event with music, food and wine.

Getting there

BY AIR

Málaga Airport

10km (6 miles) to city centre

🚇 N/A
🚌 30 minutes
🚕 25 minutes

Seville

8km (5 miles) to city centre

🚇 N/A
🚌 30 minutes
🚕 25 minutes

Most visitors to the Costa del Sol arrive at Málaga Airport (tel: 952 04 88 38), which is 10km (6 miles) outside the city centre. Spain's national airline, Iberia (tel: 902 40 05 00), operates direct scheduled flights to Málaga from major European and North American cities. The No 19 bus runs to Málaga every 30 minutes (daily 7am to 11:30pm) and takes around 30 minutes. A taxi should cost about €12.

The other nearest airport is Seville (Seville), 8km (5 miles) from the city centre (tel: 954 44 90 00), which handles internal and international flights from London, Amsterdam, Brussels and Paris. A bus into the city runs every 30 minutes (daily 6:45am to 11pm) and takes about 30 minutes. A taxi will cost you around €20.

Gibraltar Airport (tel: 956 77 30 26) is 2km (1.2 miles) from the centre of Gibraltar. There is a regular bus service to the town, and taxis are available from a taxi rank opposite the airport. Taxis to destinations throughout the Costa del Sol are available from the taxi rank on the Spanish side of the border.

BY RAIL

Málaga's main station (tel: 902 24 02 02; www.renfe.es) is just 1km (0.6 miles) from the city. However, rail journeys are very time-consuming from other parts of Europe. For example, the journey time from London is around 30 hours and you will need to change in Paris and then again at the Spanish border. You may even need to change again in Madrid. However, once in Madrid, there are a number of possible connections to Seville or Córdoba.

BY ROAD

You can drive to Spain via the Channel Tunnel (www.eurotunnel.com) and continue overland via France. The trip can take you as little as two days, but the cost of petrol, tolls and staying overnight on route can make this a costly option. There are also ferries (www.brittany-ferries.com; www.poferries.com) from England to Bilbao or Santander in Northern Spain, from where you can drive or take a train.

Getting around

PUBLIC TRANSPORT

Internal flights The national airline, Iberia, plus the smaller Spanair and Vueling airlines, operate an extensive network of internal flights. Check the websites www.iberia.com, www.spanair.com and www.vueling.com. Alternatively, Iberia and Spanair have offices at the airport. National flights are increasingly more competitively priced and are worth considering if you are in a hurry.

Trains Services are provided by the state-run company – RENFE. Fares are among the least expensive in Europe. A useful service is the coastal route from Málaga to Fuengirola, via Torremolinos and Benalmádena, with a stop at the airport. Trains run every 30 minutes between 7am and 11pm (RENFE tel: 902 24 02 02; www.renfe.es).

Buses There is a comprehensive and reliable bus network operated by different companies along the coast and to inland towns and villages. Fares are very reasonable. Go to the local bus station for details of routes. The bus station in Málaga (tel: 952 35 00 61) is just behind the RENFE train station.

Ferries A service runs from Málaga to Melilla (in Morocco), run by Trasmediterránea Málaga (tel: 902 45 46 45; www.trasmediterranea.es), taking 10 hours. A shorter route to Morocco is from Algeciras to Ceuta (1.5 hours) and Tangier – via Gibraltar – (2.5 hours) run by Trasmediterránea (tel: 956 66 52 00), and EuroFerrys (tel: 902 19 50 14; www.euroferrys.com).

Urban transport Traffic in the main towns and resorts of the Costa del Sol is normally heavy, especially in summer, but public transport in the form of buses is generally good. From the RENFE station there is a bus which runs every 10 minutes or so to the city centre.

TAXIS

Only use taxis that display a licence issued by the local authority. Taxis show a green light when available for rent. They can be flagged down in the street. In cities and large towns taxis are metered; where they are not, determine the price of the journey in advance.

DRIVING

- Drive is on the right.
- An international driving licence is required for North American visitors.
- Speed limits on *autopistas* (toll motorways) and *autovías* (free motorways): 120kph (75mph); dual carriageways and roads with overtaking lanes: 100kph (62mph). Take care on the N340 coastal highway. Cars travel at tremendous speed and this road is labelled as a dangerous one. Speed limits on country roads: 90kph (56mph). Speed limits on urban roads: 50kph (30mph); in residential areas: 20kph (12.5mph).
- Seatbelts must be worn in front seats at all times and in rear seats where fitted.
- There is random breath-testing – never drive under the influence of alcohol.
- Fuel (*gasolina*) is available as *Sin plomo* (unleaded, 95 and 98 octane) and *gasoleo* or *gasoil* (diesel). Fuel prices are fixed by the Government and are similar to those in the UK. Most stations take credit cards.
- If you break down with your own car and are a member of a motoring organization with a reciprocal agreement (such as the AA in the UK) you can contact the Real Automóvil Club de España, or RACE (tel: 902 40 45 45; www.race.es); which has English-speaking staff and offers 24-hour breakdown assistance. Most international car rental companies provide a rescue service.

CAR RENTAL

The leading international car rental companies operate on the Costa del Sol and you can rent a car in advance (essential at peak periods) either direct or through a travel agent. Airlines may offer 'fly-drive' deals. Renting from a local firm, though, is usually cheaper.

FARES, TICKETS AND CONCESSIONS

If you are staying on the Costa del Sol, especially at resorts located between Málaga and Fuengirola, you will find the half-hourly train service very useful and inexpensive, at around €2.35 for a return trip. Always buy your ticket at the machine or ticket office on the platform or you will be fined and have to pay around double on board. If the Costa is part of more widespread travel within Spain, consider purchasing a Rail Europe Spain pass that provides any three days of unlimited train travel within a two-month period at a substantial discount. Children and students also receive discounts on bus and train travel. Students must produce proof in the form of an International Student Identity Card (ISIC) or Euro 26 card. The same discount applies to entrance fees to many museums and sights which also frequently offer free admission to EU residents (take your passport).

The Costa del Sol is an excellent destination for older travellers – travel agents offer tailored package holidays. In the winter months there are special low-cost, long-stay holidays for senior citizens; the best deals are available through tour operators who specialize in holidays for senior citizens.

Being there

TOURIST OFFICES
HEAD OFFICE
● Costa del Sol Tourist Board
☎ 952 05 86 94/95;
www.visitcostadelsol.com

TOWNS/RESORTS
● Plaza San Sebastian 7, Antequera
☎ 952 70 25 05;
www.turismoantequera.com
● Avenida Antonio Machado 10,
Benalmádena Costa ☎ 952 44 12
95; www.benalmadena.com
● Avenida San Lorenzo 1,
Estepona ☎ 952 80 09 13;
www.infoestepona.com

● Avenida Jesús Santos Rein 6,
Fuengirola ☎ 952 46 74 57;
www.fuengirola.org
● Pasaje de Chinitas 4, Málaga
☎ 952 21 34 45;
www.malagaturismo.com
● Glorieta de la Fontanilla, Marbella
☎ 952 77 14 42; www.marbella.es
● Calle Puerta del Mar 4, Nerja
☎ 952 52 15 31; www.nerja.org
● Avenida Marqués del Duero 69,
San Pedro de Alcántara ☎ 952 78
52 52
● Avenida de Andalucía 52,
Torre del Mar ☎ 952 54 11 04
● Ayuntamiento, Plaza Picasso,
Torremolinos ☎ 952 37 95 12;
www.ayto-torremolinos.org

MONEY
Spain's currency is the euro (€), which is divided into 100 cents. Coins
come in denominations of 1, 2, 5, 10, 20 and 50 cents, €1 and €2, and
notes come in denominations of €5, €10, €20, €50, €100, €200 and €500.
Euro traveller's cheques may be exchanged in banks and exchange offices
but the commission may be high and they are not generally acccepted for
purchases. Credit cards are widely acccepted.

TIPS/GRATUITIES

Yes ✓ No ✗		
Restaurants (if service not included)	✓	5–10%
Cafés/bars	✓	change
Taxis	✓	change
Porters	✓	change
Chambermaids	✓	change
Toilets	✓	change

POSTAL AND INTERNET SERVICES

Post offices *(correos)* are generally open as below; in main centres they may open extended hours. Málaga's main post office is at Avenida de Andalucía 1. Stamps *(sellos)* can also be bought at tobacconists *(estancos)*. Open: Mon–Sat 9–2 (1pm Sat), tel: 902 29 72 97 (Málaga).

Internet cafés are located throughout Andalucía and the local tourist office should be able to provide you with a list. The approximate cost of an hour's internet use is €3–€4. Better quality hotels should provide WiFi coverage, at least in the lobby, plus the available plug in the room for those guests travelling with a laptop.

TELEPHONES

All telephone numbers in Spain consist of nine digits. Most public telephones take coins and phonecards *(tarjetas telefónicas)*, which are sold at *tabacos* or post offices for €6 or €12. Some accept credit cards.

Emergency telephone numbers

Police: (Policía Nacional) 112;
(Policía Local) 092
Ambulance: (Ambulancia) 061

Fire: (Bomberos) 080 or
952 12 66 00 (Málaga);
952 77 43 49 (Marbella);
952 38 39 39 (Torremolinos)

International dialling codes

UK: 00 44
Germany: 00 49

USA/Canada: 00 1
Netherlands: 00 31

EMBASSIES AND CONSULATES

UK ☎ 952 35 23 00 (Málaga)
Germany ☎ 952 36 35 91 (Málaga)
USA ☎ 952 47 48 91 (Fuengirola)

Ireland ☎ 952 47
51 08 (Fuengirola)

HEALTH AND SAFETY

Sun advice The sunniest (and hottest) months are July and August. Try to avoid the midday sun and use a high-factor sun block at first, and allow yourself to become used to the sun gradually. Protective hats are advisable.

Drugs Prescriptions and non-prescription drugs and medicines are available from pharmacies *(farmácias)*, distinguished by a large green cross. They are able to dispense many drugs which would be available only on prescription in other countries.

Safe water Tap water is generally safe to drink; however, unfamiliar water may cause mild abdominal upsets. Mineral water *(agua mineral)* is cheap and widely available. It is sold *sin gas* (still) and *con gas* (carbonated).

Petty crime Snatching of handbags and cameras, pick-pocketing, theft of unattended baggage and car break-ins are the principal crimes against visitors. Any crime or loss should be reported to the national police force (Policía Nacional), who wear brown uniforms. Take the same precautions as you would at home.

ELECTRICITY

The power supply is: 220/230 volts (in some bathrooms and older buildings: 110/120 volts).

Round, two-hole sockets take round plugs with two round pins. British visitors will need an adaptor and US visitors a transformer.

OPENING HOURS

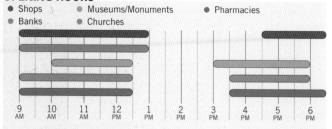

In addition to the times above, department stores, larger super-markets and shops in tourist resorts open from 10am through to 8, 9 or even 10pm. Most shops close Sunday and some in August. Most banks open 9–2 (Mon–Fri). Some banks also open Sat 9–2 (Oct–May). The opening times of museums can vary: some open longer in summer, while hours may be reduced in winter. Many museums close Sunday afternoon, some on Saturday afternoon, as well as Monday or another day in the week.

LANGUAGE

Spanish is one of the easiest languages. All vowels are pure and short (as in English). Some useful tips on speaking: 'c' is lisped before 'e' and 'i', otherwise hard; 'h' is silent; 'j' is pronounced like a gutteral 'j'; 'r' is rolled; 'v' sounds more like 'b'; and 'z' is the same as a soft 'c'. English is widely spoken in the principal resorts but you will get a better reception if you at least try communicating with Spaniards in their own tongue.

yes/no	*sí/no*	help!	*ayuda!*
please/thank you	*por favor/gracias*	today/tomorrow	*hoy/mañana*
hello/goodbye	*hola/adiós*	yesterday	*ayer*
good night	*buenas noches*	how much?	*¿cuánto?*
excuse me	*perdóneme*	open/closed	*abierto/cerrado*
hotel	hotel	reservation/rate	reserva/precio
room	habitación	breakfast	desayuno
single/double	individual/doble	toilet	lavabo
one/two nights	una/dos noche(s)	bath/shower	baño'ducha
per person/per room	por persona/por habitación	key	llave
		chambermaid	camarera
bank/cashier	banco/cajero	foreign currency	moneda extranjera
exchange office	oficina de cambio	bank card	tarjeta del banco
post office	correos	credit card	tarjeta de crédito
money/coin	dinero/moneda	traveller's cheque	cheque de viajero
restaurant/bar	*restaurante/bar*	starter	*primer plato*
table/menu	*mesa/carta*	dish/main course	*plato/plato principal*
tourist menu	*menú turístico*	dessert/drink	*postre/bebida*
wine list	*carta de vinos*	waiter	*camarero*
lunch/dinner	*almuerzo/cena*	bill	*cuenta*
plane/airport	*avión/aeropuerto*	ferry/port	*transbordador/puerto*
train/train station	*tren/estación de ferrocarril*	ticket	*billete*
		... single/return	*ida/ida y vuelta*
bus/bus station	*autobús/estación de autobuses*	timetable	*horario*
		seat	*asiento*

Best places to see

1 La Alcazaba, Málaga

The old Moorish fortress, or Alcazaba, dating back to the second half of the 11th century, stands high above the city of Málaga.

Just up from the Plaza de Aduana are the solid, fortified walls of La Alcazaba, the landmark of Málaga. It dates back to the 700s, but most of the structure belongs to the mid-11th century. Entrance is through the gateway known as the Puerta del Cristo (Christ's Door), where the first Mass was celebrated following the Christian victory over the town.

The way winds up through attractive gardens, fountains and courtyards, passing through the gateways of Puerta de las Columnas, Arco del Cristo and Arcos de Granada. The terraces have magnificent views of the town and harbour. A small palace within the inner perimeter is the home of the Museo de la Alcazaba, which displays a range of Moorish objects recovered from the area.

Below the Alcazaba are the 2nd-century ruins of a Roman amphitheatre. Much of the original structure can be seen, with explanation plaques in English. Occasional performances are staged here. Above the Alcazaba stands the castle which crowns the Gibralfaro Hill (➤ 85).

✚ *Málaga 6c* ✉ Calle Alcazabilla, s/n ☎ 952 22 51 06 🕒 Apr–Sep Tue–Sun 9:30–8; Oct–Mar Tue–Sun 8:30–7 ✋ Inexpensive ¶¶ Many nearby 🚉 Centro-Alameda railway station

2 La Alhambra, Granada

One of Spain's greatest splendours, the palace of La Alhambra remains as a legacy of the rich culture brought to the peninsula by the Moors.

The Alhambra holds a commanding position above the city of Granada, backed by the snowcapped peaks of the Sierra Nevada. Built by the Moors between the 13th and 15th centuries, it was used as a residence by Muhammad I, and members of the Nasrid dynasty. In 1984 it joined UNESCO's list of World Heritage Sites.

Walk up to the entrance from the Plaza Nueva. To the east is the Renaissance palace of Emperor Carlos V, started in 1526 but never completed. To the west is the Alcazaba, the oldest building on the site. Climb to the top of the Vela tower for breathtaking views of Granada and the Sierra Nevada.

A tour of the interior of the Casa Real (Royal Palace) reveals the true marvels: the beautifully decorated Patio de Mexuar, the pretty Patio de los Arrayanes (named after the myrtle trees that line a rectangular pool), and the Salón de los Embajadores (Ambassadors' Hall) with its richly carved and coffered ceiling. The Sala de los Abencerrajes has an impressive stalactite ceiling, and the Sala de las Dos Hermanas (Hall of the Two Sisters) features a delicate honeycomb dome. The focal point is the Patio de los Leones (Courtyard of Lions), named after the figures around the fountain.

On the nearby Cerro del Sol (Hill of the Sun) stands the Palacio del Generalife. Dating back to the early 1300s, it was the summer palace of the Moorish kings. The gardens exude an aura of romance, with pools and fountains amid greenery, flowers and the resident cats.

🞥 24J ✉ Calle Real, s/n, Granada ☎ 902 44 12 21
🕓 Mar–Oct daily 8:30–8. Night visits Tue–Sat 10–11:30, Fri, Sat 8–9:30. Access to the Palacios Nazaries 8am–8:45pm 👖 Moderate; free Sun after 3pm for visitors with disabilities, senior citizens 🍴 Few 🚌 Alhambrabus from town centre ❓ Booking is essential as only a limited number of tickets are sold daily on site but sell out quickly. Book either via www.alhambratickets.com or through branches of Banco Bilbao Vizcaya Argentaria (BBV)

3 Casares

With its mass of whitewashed houses sprawling up the hillside, Casares has acquired a reputation for being the most photogenic town in Andalucía.

From whichever angle you approach, the views of Casares are spectacular. The town is easily accessible from the coast: a turning around 16km (10 miles) west of Estepona leads up into the hills of the Sierra Bermeja. While the drive itself takes you through a scenic route of hills and wooded areas, nothing prepares you for the spectacular

view of Casares with its white houses spread over the hill crowned by a Moorish castle. The town saw many battles between the warring Muslims, until it was taken by the Christians in the mid-15th century.

Much of the charm of Casares can be discovered by strolling through its terraced streets to the castle above. On the way up, take a look at the 17th-century Church of San Sebastian, which contains a statue of the Virgen del Rosario del Campo. The castle was built in the 13th century on Roman foundations. The nearby 16th-century Church of the Incarnation retains its original Mudéjar tower.

The views become more spectacular as you continue to the summit, where you will be rewarded by a panorama over olive groves, orchards and forests stretching to the blue of the Mediterranean Sea. Take a look at the local cemetery, which is beautifully kept and adorned with flowers.

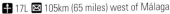

✚ 17L ✉ 105km (65 miles) west of Málaga
🍴 Several restaurants 🚌 Local buses
❓ August Fair (early Aug)
ℹ Calle Villa 29, Casares ☎ 952 89 41 26

4 Casco Antiguo, Marbella

The jewel of Marbella is its Casco Antiguo (Old Town), a picturesque maze of narrow streets, whitewashed houses and pretty squares.

To the north of central Avenida Ramón y Cajal, Marbella's old quarter is a delightful area for strolling with its flower-filled streets, whitewashed houses and small squares. Among its prettiest streets are Calle Dolores, Calle Ortiz de Molinillos and San Cristóbal, noted for the brilliance of their flower displays.

Sooner or later everyone converges on the Plaza de los Naranjos, a lovely square lined with orange trees. This is a popular place for a drink or alfresco meal where you can enjoy people-watching and the streetlife. In the middle of the square is a bust of a serene King Juan Carlos.

Evidence of the town's Moorish, Christian and Roman past can be seen on many of its buildings. Take a look at the church of Nuestra Señora de la Encarnación and, above it, the remaining towers of an old Moorish fortress; the 16th-century Ayuntamiento (Town Hall), home of the main tourist office, the Casa Consistorial, which has a fine Mudéjar entrance and the 15th-century Ermita de Nuestro Señor Santiago, Marbella's earliest Christian church. Worth a glimpse, too, is the attractive little Cofradía del Santo Christo de Amor chapel, at one end of the plaza. A stroll through this area is particularly enjoyable in spring when the heady scent of orange blossom fills the air.

✠ 18L ✉ Marbella (56km/35 miles west of Málaga)
🍴 Many restaurants (€–€€€) 🚌 Marbella bus stop,
Avenida Ricardo Soriano 21 (Bus station Avenida Trapiche,
s/n) ❓ Pre-Lent Carnival; Fería de San Bernabé (11–18 Jun)

5 Cuevas de Nerja

This series of caverns, close to the coastal town of Nerja, has spectacular rock formations and palaeolithic paintings.

These limestone caves were discovered by chance in 1959 by a group of boys who were out and about exploring. Beyond the first grotto, great caverns revealed a wonderful world of stalactites and stalagmites, and various items such as stone tools and fragments of pottery. Investigations show that the area must have been inhabited by man more than 20,000 years ago. A group of sculptures near the entrance to the caves honours the boys who made the discovery.

The rock paintings of horses, deer, goats and dolphins are not open for public viewing, but photographs of them are on display, together with

objects found here. However, the main attraction is the display of formations enhanced by special lighting effects.

The first chamber provides a magnificent setting for classical music and dance concerts, which are held here as part of an annual summer festival. The next cavern is called the Hall of Ghosts after a strange shroud-like figure that appears in the stone. Most impressive is the huge Cataclysm Hall, which features the tallest column of its kind in the world, rising from a mass of stalactites.

🕂 22L 🖂 4km (2.5 miles) east of Nerja ☎ 952 52 95 20 🕔 Jul–Aug daily 10–9:30; Sep–Jun daily 10–2 4–6:30 👋 Inexpensive 🍽 Restaurant (€€) 🚇 Best by car ❓ Summer concerts and ballet performances

6 La Giralda y La Catedral, Sevilla

The minaret tower known as La Giralda, seen as a symbol of Sevilla, rises proudly above the great cathedral, the third largest in Europe.

The 98m-high (320ft) brick tower of La Giralda is a prominent feature of Sevilla. It was built in the 12th century as the minaret of the former Great Mosque. In 1565 a section with 25 bells was added and topped with a bronze statue representing Faith, which acts as a *giralda* (weather vane). Climb up to the belfry for magnificent views over the city. Note that there are ramps, not stairs, so it is relatively easy on the knees.

The grand cathedral was built in the Gothic style, with some Renaissance influences. The interior is awe-inspiring for its sheer size and the richness of its decoration, with Gothic columns supporting massive arches that reach up to the great heights of the vaulted ceiling.

A handsome 16th-century grille in the Sanctuary encloses an immense golden Gothic altarpiece which rates as one of the cathedral's greatest glories and is said to be the largest altar in the world. Started by the Flemish artist Dancart in 1482, it took almost a hundred years to complete the 45 tableaux depicting the lives of Jesus and Mary.

The choirstalls are fine examples of Flamboyant Gothic. Notable also is the Capilla Real (Royal Chapel); completed in 1575, it features a richly decorated Renaissance cupola. On either side are the tombs of King Alfonso X (the Wise) and his mother, Beatrice of Swabia. In the south transept is the ornate tomb of Christopher Columbus, whose body lay here after it was transported from Cuba.

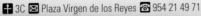

✚ 3C ✉ Plaza Virgen de los Reyes ☎ 954 21 49 71
🕐 Jul–Aug Mon–Sat 9:30–3:30, Sun 2:30–6; Sep–Jun Mon–Sat 11–5, Sun 2–6 💰 Moderate; Sun free 🍴 Many restaurants nearby 🚊 RENFE station
ℹ️ Sevilla (▶ 133)

7

La Mezquita, Córdoba

The great mosque of Córdoba stands as a remarkable achievement and monument to Moorish architecture.

The Mezquita of Córdoba was built in four stages between the 8th and 10th centuries and is among the world's largest mosques, remaining as a testimony to the immense power of Islam at the height of its domination of the peninsula.

Do not be discouraged by the mosque's somewhat forbidding outward appearance: its beauty lies within. The main entrance is through the

Puerta del Perdón, which leads into the Patio de los Naranjos (Courtyard of the Oranges). Once inside you are confronted by a forest of columns of onyx, marble and granite. The light effects within this dim interior are sensational. The columns are topped by decorated capitals and crowned by the striking red and white arches so characteristic of Moorish architecture. There is a sense of awe and mysticism, special to this particular mosque, which lures the visitor back time and time again.

To find a Christian cathedral within the very heart of the mosque comes as a surprise. It was built in the 1520s on the orders of Hapsburg Emperor Carlos V, who later regretted his decision. However, it does blend fairly well into its surroundings.

Rising above the Puerta del Perdón is the bell tower, which offers splendid views of the city.

✚ 9B ✉ Torrijos y Cardenal Herrero ☎ 957 47 05 12 🕐 Mar, Jul–Oct Mon–Sat 10–6:30, 8:30–9:45, Sun 2–6:30; Feb, Nov Mon–Sat 10–5:30, Sun 2–5:30; Dec–Jan Mon–Sat 10–5, Sun 8:30–9:45, 2–5; Apr–Jun Mon–Sat 8:30–9:45, Sun 2–7 💷 Moderate 🍴 Many restaurants nearby (€–€€€) 🚆 RENFE station, Avenida de America, Córdoba ℹ Córdoba (➤ 111)

8 Mijas

With its attractive mountain setting, narrow streets and whitewashed houses, Mijas is a popular excursion from the coast.

Despite the fact that Mijas caters so obviously for the tourist it has retained its charm, with its white houses, narrow winding streets, flowers and plants. The setting is lovely, with magnificent views of the surrounding pine-clad mountains and the sea. Its proximity to the coast, a drive of some 20 minutes or so, makes it an ideal destination for a day's excursion.

The village's origins date back to the Moors, and the most central church, the Iglesia de la Concepción Inmaculada, was built in the 17th century on the site of a former mosque. More recently, several ancient wall paintings were discovered here during renovation.

Just beyond the main car park is a cave which serves as a shrine to the village's patroness, La Virgen de la Peña (Shrine of the Virgin of the Rock). Apparently the Virgin Mary appeared to a daughter of the family who once lived here. To commemorate the event, a tiny image of the Virgin is kept here, thought to date back to AD850.

Keep looking and you may just spy a hang-glider wafting overhead. This is a popular sport in the area. There is also a thriving arts and crafts movement in Mijas, particularly linen and wicker

items, and the locally made bread and honey are definitely worth trying.

Concerts and fiestas are sometimes held in the main square, which centres around a small fountain and is a popular meeting place.

✚ 19L ✉ 37km (23 miles) west of Málaga 🍴 Many restaurants (€–€€€) 🚍 Local bus services ❓ St Anthony's Day (16–17 Jan); Fería de la Virgen de la Peña (early Sep); Romería de Santa Teresa (end Oct)

ℹ Ayuntamiento, Plaza Virgen de la Peña, s/n
☎ 952 58 90 34

9 Puente Nuevo, Ronda

The old town of Ronda is famed for its spectacular setting and views from the bridge over the El Tajo ravine.

Ronda is one of Spain's oldest cities. Situated within the rugged landscape of the Serranía de Ronda, the town is split in two, divided by the gorge of the River Guadalevín, which is spanned by the Puente Nuevo (New Bridge). The city has long held a deep fascination with writers and painters and the scene of Ronda perched on the clifftop with the bridge spanning the gorge has been the subject of countless paintings and photographs. Today, the dramatic views from the bridge, combined with the attractions of the old town and its historical interest, continue to make Ronda (➤ 124–125) a top excursion for visitors staying along the coast.

The Puente Nuevo (which has become the city's symbol) was begun in 1751 and completed in 1793. It stands a full 96m (315ft) above the Tajo gorge at its highest and narrowest point. Sadly, the bridge's architect did not live to see its completion, tragically dying after falling out of a basket while inspecting its construction.

✚ 17J ✉ 118km (73 miles) northwest of Málaga
🍽 Many restaurants in Ronda (€–€€€) 🚌 Buses from Algeciras, Cádiz, Málaga (via Torremolinos, Marbella, San Pedro) and Sevilla
ℹ Ronda (➤ 125)

10 Puerto Banús

The dazzling marina of Puerto Banús, with its luxurious yachts and sophisticated restaurants and bars, serves as a magnet for visitors to the Costa del Sol.

A stay on the Costa del Sol would be incomplete without a visit to Puerto Banús, one of the Costa's most famous attractions. Built in 1968, this luxurious port, the creation of promoter José Banús, was one of Spain's first village-type harbour developments.

Backed by the mountains, a ring of brilliant white apartment houses surrounds the marina, which is

filled with craft of all sizes, from mega yachts to small sailing boats. A feature of Banús is the complex of luxury apartments, located on the right as you enter the port. With its opulent marble facade and gleaming turrets, the inspiration could have been taken straight from the *Arabian Nights*.

Around the port is a string of cafés, bars and restaurants, along with boutiques and gift shops. While frontline restaurants are *the* places in which to be seen, better value is sometimes found in some of the small restaurants in the streets behind, tucked away up flights of stairs. In season the quayside is thronged with people who come to see, or to be seen – this can be a great place for celebrity-spotting. The Saladuba Pub and the Sinatra Bar are favourite haunts for hanging out.

At night the place becomes a hive of activity, as the smart restaurants, slick piano bars and clubs fill up with the chichi set. While the glamour of its earlier days may have dimmed, Banús still rates as a star attraction.

✚ 18L ✉ 64km (40 miles) west of Málaga, 6km (4 miles) west of Marbella 🍴 Many bars and restaurants (€€–€€€) 🚌 Bus services from Marbella and San Pedro de Alcántara ℹ Avenida Principal, s/n ☎ 952 11 38 30 (summer only)

Best things to do

Good places to have lunch

La Alcazaba (€€)

Enjoys a prime position with panoramic views that stretch to Morocco on a clear day. The traditional Spanish menu includes *ajo blanco* (almond and garlic soup), paella and fish and meat dishes.

✉ Plaza de la Constitución, Mijas ☎ 952 59 02 53

El Balcón de la Virgen (€€)

The lovely terrace here is overlooked by a 200-year-old statue of the Virgin surrounded by bougainvillaea. The hearty menu includes meat and fish dishes such as roast pork and marinated swordfish.

✉ Remedios 2, Marbella ☎ 952 77 60 92

Casa Juan (€€)

An institution among locals who flock here on weekends to sample the legendary fresh seafood. There's outside seating in the pretty square, a block back from the beach.

✉ Plaza San Gines, La Carihuela ☎ 952 37 35 12

Casa Luque (€€)

Although housed in a delightful old Andalucían house, the cuisine is from the north of Spain, with an emphasis on meat and game.

✉ Plaza Cavana 2, Nerja ☎ 952 52 10 04

Pitta Bar (€)

Ideally placed between the Museo Picasso and the cathedral, this Middle Eastern restaurant has outside tables and dishes up traditional fare such as falafel, humous, tabouleh and kebabs.

✉ Echegaray 8, Málaga ☎ 952 60 86 75

Restaurante Antonio (€€)

One of the Port's best restaurants overlooking the water. The speciality is sea bass baked in salt.

✉ Calle Muelle Rivera, Puerto Banús ☎ 952 81 35 36

Santiago (€€)

This sunny dining space in a pleasant position on the seafront, is said to be one of Marbella's top restaurants for fish and seafood.

✉ Paseo Marítimo 5, Marbella ☎ 952 77 00 78

Tintero (€)

An entertaining seafood restaurant with a vast terrace. There is no menu, instead waiters circle the tables carrying plates of food and you select what you fancy; the bill is totted up by counting the number of the plates at the end of your meal.

✉ Carretera Almería, El Palo ☎ 607 60 75 86

Vegetalia (€)

The vegetarian lunchtime buffet here is excellent value, with a vast choice including salads and hot dishes such as lentil burgers and *seitan* cutlets. Leave room for the blueberry pie.

✉ Santa Isabel 8, Los Boliches, Fuengirola ☎ 952 58 60 31

Yate El Cordobes (€)

Locals flock to this good *chiringuito* on the beach. The *salmorejo* (thick gazpacho with chopped ham and egg) is recommended.

✉ Paseo Marítimo Playamar, Torremolinos ☎ 952 38 49 56
🕐 Closed Nov–Apr

Activities

Golf
This stretch of coast is often described as the Costa del Golf. In fact golf has a tremendous impact on the Costa del Sol area. Its mild winter climate, combined with an abundance of high-quality courses, make it a highly desirable year-round golfing destination. It was a matter of great pride that the Valderrama Golf Course in Sotogrande was the first course outside the UK and US to host the Ryder Cup in 1997. Since then, the region has hosted numerous international golfing events.

Horse-back riding
In the land of great horse-handling and riding, what else should you do? There are excellent equestrian establishments up and down the coast and in the hills.

In the air
Introduced a few years ago, flysurfing, or kitesurfing, has become a lifestyle for some throughout the Costa del Sol, although in reality the winds here are rarely sufficiently breezy and serious 'surfers' head for Tarifa on the Costa de la Luz. Hot-air ballooning, gliding, para-gliding and hang-gliding are all popular.

Sailing
The numerous marinas dotted along the coast have excellent sailing facilities. Most of the marinas and their yacht clubs organize beginners' sailing, monitor and yacht-master classes in summer. Major marinas include: La Duquesa, Estepona, Marbella, Fuengirola, Benalmádena and Málaga.

Scuba diving
Almuñécar and Nerja, east of Málaga, are good diving centres. Day courses with fully qualified instructors are available at various places along the coast.

Skiing
The Sierra Nevada ski station is only 100km (60 miles) from the coast. Facilities include good transport, ski lifts, chair lifts and a tourist complex. Season is from December to April.

Swimming
Beaches are closely monitored for cleanliness, with the result that many display the coveted Blue Flag – classified by 5 to 1 stars. Some inland villages have local swimming pools.

Tennis
Most top hotels along the coast have tennis courts, especially in and around Marbella; hotel guests have priority in renting the courts. There are also a number of tennis clubs in the area.

Waterskiing and windsurfing
There are plenty of opportunities for waterskiing and windsurfing along the western coast of the Costa del Sol. Facilities and tuition are available in all major resorts, often from the hotels. For kitesurfing, head for Tarifa.

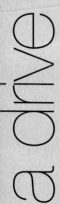

a drive

up into the hills to Mijas

This drive takes you up into the hills through attractive scenery to the picturesque village of Mijas, passing a couple of other typical Andalucian villages on the return to the coast.

From Benalmádena Costa take the N340 east for a short distance. Turn inland, following the sign to Arroyo de la Miel. In the village turn left at the traffic lights and follow the signs to Tivoli World. Continue up the hill and pass by the Tivoli World amusement park on your right, continuing to Benalmádena Pueblo. Proceed straight through the village and follow the signs to Mijas.

A winding road (with some bad stretches and narrow sections) takes you through pine-clad hillls, with fine views down to the coast. You should reach Mijas some 30 minutes later.

Take the A387 northwest to Alhaurín el Grande, 17km (10.5 miles) on.

Drive on through a winding stretch of reddish rocks and pines, with some fine panoramic views on your left, and bear right, continuing on the A387 to the village of Alhaurín el Grande. Look for the signs and join the A366 northwest to Coín, which you should reach some 10 minutes later.

After Coín, turn onto the A355, following the signs for Ojén-Marbella, to Monda. Continue on the A355, which now heads south towards Ojén-Marbella.

The road from here to Ojén has a good surface and continuing curves as it passes through an area of rocks

BEST THINGS TO DO

and wooded hills. It will take you some 45 minutes to reach Ojén.

Continue south for 8km (5 miles) to the N340 coastal road and take the AP7 toll road (exit Arroyo de la Miel) in the direction of Málaga back to Benalmádena Costa.

Distance 116km (72 miles)
Time About 5 hours, allowing time to visit Mijas
Start/end point Benalmádena Costa ✚ 20L
Lunch El Mirlo Blanco (€€) ✉ Plaza de la Constitución, Mijas
☎ 952 48 57 00 ⓒ Closed Jan

Peace and quiet

Within reach of the coast are a number of protected areas and nature parks with landscapes of wild beauty and a wealth of flora and fauna, making an ideal destination for the nature lover.

Los Alcornocales
This unspoiled landscape inland from Tarifa harbours one of the world's largest areas of cork oak forest. There is also a chance of spotting golden eagles, vultures and deer.

Las Alpujarras
Lying between the coastal sierras of Lujar, La Contraviesa, Gador and the Sierra Nevada is the region of Las Alpujarras, whose remoteness and inaccessibility has provided cover for fugitives in the past. For the Moors who fled here after the fall of Granada, and the legendary bandits and Republicans who sought refuge here after the civil war, the region has played its role. It now has a growing appeal to expatriates seeking a different sort of retreat.

Laguna de Fuente de Piedra
Located off the N334 west of Antequera, this area of exceptional beauty is known as the Pink Lagoon, after a large colony of flamingoes that comes here every year to breed; the best time to see these spectacular birds is from the end of January to June. The chicks hatch around April and May.

Parque Nacional Coto de Doñana
The park is an important resting area for a variety of migratory birds that lies on the Atlantic seaboard to the west of Cádiz, and comprises the vast area of marshland and dunes of the delta of the River Guadalquivir. It is one of Europe's largest wetland areas.
✉ Visitor Centre ☎ 959 44 87 11; www.parquenacionaldonana.com

Parque Natural Sierra Nevada
This huge area of high land southeast of Granada contains the area's highest peak, Mulhacén. It is famed for its scenery and diversity of plant and animal life.

Parque Natural Torcal de Antequera
This national park, south of Antequera, has wonderful rock formations.
✉ Visitor Centre ☎ 952 03 13 89

Rural Retreats
A short distance from the coast are a number of rural lodgings in wonderful scenery, which can vary from country cottages, rooms in *haciendas* to mountain refuges or hostels.

For information and reservations:
RAAR (Red Andaluza de Alojamientos Rurales)
✉ Sagunto 8–10, 04004 Almeria ☎ 902 44 22 33; www.raar.es

You can also contact:
Asociación de Hoteles Rurales de Andalucía
✉ Avenida Niceto Alcalá, Priego de Córdoba
☎ 957 54 08 01; www.ahra.es
Rural Andalus
✉ Calle Montes de Oca 18, 29007 Málaga
☎ 952 27 62 29; www.ruralandalus.es

Beaches

Bajondillo
In the middle of Torremolinos, accessed down steep steps through the old fishing district of Bajondillo, this is a lively beach frequented by locals. The clean wide sands are well serviced and backed by massive hotels, apartment blocks, bars and restaurants. To the right beyond the rocks lies the beach area of La Carihuela, famed for its seafood restaurants.

Cala de Maro
Just east of Nerja, the pines trees provide a wild and exotic feel. A parking area is available but it fills up quickly.

La Cala
Lying between Fuengirola and Marbella, this quiet Blue Flag beach is perfect for families and couples. Relax in one of the beach bars and watch the sun go down as the kids play safely nearby.

Playa de Los Boliches
There is something for everyone at this central Fuengirola beach, one of the longest in the area at 1,000m (1,090yds). It is well equipped, offering restaurants, hotels, shops and sports. A favourite spot, although it can be very crowded.

Playa de Fuengirola
Another popular Fuengirola beach that sits between Los Boliches beach and the one at Santa Amalia. It is near the Fuengirola castle, which is open to the public.

Playa de Los Lances
This sweeping white sandy beach due west of Tarifa is refreshingly free of rows of rental sunbeds (bring your own) and is popular with wind- and kitesurfers. On a clear day you can see Africa across the water.

La Rada

Estepona's expansive stretch of fine sand is right in the heart of town and west of the marina. It is clean and safe with good facilities (Blue Flag). Beach bars/restaurants serving traditional Spanish food front the attractive promenade.

Santa Ana

One of Benalmádena's many Blue Flag beaches with plenty of facilities and lots to do. The 500m (545yds) of golden sands are fairly crowded, particularly in summer. An artificial dyke separates the Santa Ana beach from that of Torre Bermeja.

La Vibora

Between Benalmádena and Fuengirola in a semi-urban location, La Vibora is next to the stream of the same name. The 650m (709yd) beach has clean golden sand and tends to be less crowded than some of the lively resort beaches, but still offers good facilities, including two beach bars, a beach club and water sports.

Places to take the children

Aqualand

Aquatic attractions include giant water chutes, water mountains and artificial waves.

✉ Carretera de Circunvalación (near Palacio de Congresos), Torremolinos
☎ 952 38 88 88; www.aqualand.es 🕐 May–Sep daily 10–6 ✋ Expensive
🍴 Restaurant 🚉 RENFE station Torremolinos 🚌

Crocodile Park

The park has more than 300 crocodiles of all ages and sizes. Guided visits with a crocodile trainer. Children under 12 must be accompanied by an adult.

✉ Calle Cuba, 14 Torremolinos ☎ 952 05 17 82; www.crocodile-park.com
🕐 Summer daily 10–7; winter daily 10–5 ✋ Moderate 🅿 Nearby

Cuevas de Nerja

These caves were discovered in 1959 by schoolboys looking for bats. Resembling an enormous underground cathedral there are impressive stalactites, stalag-mites and rock formations (► 44–45).

✉ Carretera de Maro ☎ 952 52 95 20
🕐 Jul–Aug daily 10–2, 4–8; Sep–Jun daily 10–2, 4–6:30 ✋ Moderate

Parklandia

This small, colourful amusement park has a maze, trampolines, mini-racetrack, electric train, bouncy castle and more.

✉ Fuengirola port ☎ 952 58 12 86
🕐 Summer daily 10–8; winter daily 10–5 ✋ Inexpensive

Parque Acuático Mijas

Water theme park with great watershoots, including a thrilling
Kamikaze, slides and rapids.

✉ Carretera N340, Km290, Fuengirola ☎ 952 46 04 09; www.aquamijas.com
🕐 May daily 10–5:30; Jun, Sep daily 10–6; Jul, Aug daily 10–7; closed
Oct–Apr 🖐 Expensive 🍴 Restaurant (€€) 🚌 Fuengirola bus station

Sea Life Benalmádena

Enjoy close views of marine life. There are feeding displays and
presentations. An area on the sea horse is a delightful addition.

✉ Puerto Deportivo, Benalmádena ☎ 952 56 01 50; www.sealife.es
🕐 Daily 10–6 🖐 Moderate 🍴 Restaurant (€€) 🚉 RENFE station
Benalmádena-Arroyo de la Miel

Selwo Aventura

A safari park where you can see a whole range of animals from
the five continents, roaming in a semi-wild habitat. Much of the
circuit is made by safari-style jeep.

✉ Autovía Costa del Sol, Km162.5, Las Lomas del Monte ☎ 902 19 04 82;
www.selwo.es 🕐 Jan–May, Oct–Dec daily 10–6; Jun–Sep daily 10–7
🖐 Expensive 🚌 Direct to Selwo (Costa line)

Selwo Marina

This park has Andalucía's first dolphinarium and penguinarium.
Exhibitions feature dolphins, sea lions and exotic birds.

✉ Parque de la Paloma, s/n Benalmádena ☎ 902 19 04 82;
www.selwomarina.com 🕐 Daily 10–6 🖐 Moderate

Zoo Fuengirola

Spectacular modern zoo that re-creates the natural habitat of all
the species here.

✉ Camolio José Cela 6, Fuengirola ☎ 952 66 63 01;
www.zoofuengirola.com 🕐 Daily 10–6 🖐 Moderate
🚉 RENFE station Fuengirola

Stunning views

Alcazaba and Gibralfaro
Walk up Gibralfaro Hill to the castle that tops the Alcazaba and has amazing panoramic views of Málaga (➤ 36–37, 85).

La Alhambra, Granada
Climb the Vela tower for breathtaking views of Granada and the Sierra Nevada (➤ 38–39).

Balcón de Europa, Nerja
Nerja's palm-lined promontory on the old belvedere of an original fortress has spectacular coastal views (➤ 176).

Benalmádena Cable Car
This four-person cable car, near to Tivoli World, carries you to the summit of the Calamorro Mountain. There are panoramic views of the coast and the Málaga mountains.

Casares
Nothing prepares you for the view of Casares as you approach the town from the mountain roads (➤ 40–41).

Gaucín
From Eagle's Castle high above the village you can enjoy one of the best views of the Rock of Gibraltar out across the valley (➤ 116–117).

Mijas
Drive up into the hills to Mijas and enjoy the magnificent views of the pine-clad mountains and the coast below (➤ 50–51).

Puerto Banús

As you quench your thirst in a waterfront bar the mountains form a wonderful backdrop for the luxurious yachts across the water (➤ 54–55).

Ronda's Puente Nuevo

Come here for spectacular views of the ravine below and the surrounding landscape (➤ 52–53).

Hill towns and villages

Antequera
Well worth a visit, Antequera is an interesting old town with many churches, convents and squares (➤ 104–105).

Casares
The sight of Casares sprawling over the hillside in a cluster of white houses is always breathtaking (➤ 40–41).

Cómpeta
There are many different aspects to the typically Andalucian village of Cómpeta (➤ 169).

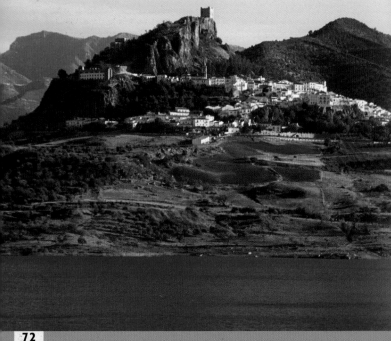

Frigiliana

This beautiful village with cobbled streets and whitewashed houses lies nestled in the hills above Nerja (➤ 170–171).

Gaucín

The small town of Gaucín nestles below a great rock massif crowned by an ancient Moorish castle (➤ 116–117).

Mijas

Delightful village noted for its hillside setting and pretty whitewashed houses (➤ 50–51).

Ojén

Drive up into the hills to the quiet little village of Ojén, a typical Andalucían white village with narrow winding roads. There is a wonderful parish church in the pretty market place and a wine museum where you can take a tour and sample the goods.

✉ About 10km (6 miles) north of Marbella

Ronda

Ronda's gorge spanned by the Puente Nuevo is the town's dominant feature (➤ 124–125).

Zahara de la Sierra

Hailed as one of the finest of the *pueblos blancos* (white towns) in the area, Zahara de la Sierra occupies a spectacular hilltop position. The red-roofed, gleaming white houses of the village are set against the backdrop of a Moorish castle in the Sierra Margarita.

✉ 22km (13.5 miles) northwest of Ronda

Zuheros

Traditional village of narrow streets and whitewashed houses, set high up on a rocky hillside in the Sierra Subbética range (➤ 183).

Marinas

Top street markets

Selling a variety of goods, ranging from handicrafts and clothes to fruit and vegetables, these *mercados* are fun to browse around.

Monday: Marbella, by the football stadium

Tuesday: Fuengirola
✉ Avenida Jesús Santo Rein, Recinto Ferial and Nerja
✉ Antonio Ferrandiz Chanquete

Wednesday: Estepona
✉ Avenida Juan Carlos

Thursday: San Pedro de Alcántara (Arquillo district)

Friday: Benalmádena
✉ Arroyo de Miel

Saturday: Nueva Andalucía
✉ The Bullring

Sunday: Estepona
✉ The Port

Best places to see flamenco

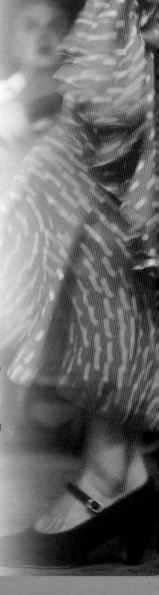

BENALMÁDENA COSTA
Fortuna Nightclub
International-calibre cabaret, flamenco and dancing to live bands.
✉ Casino Torrequebrada, N340 between Benalmádena Costa and Carvaja ☎ 952 44 60 00
🕐 From 10:30pm with dinner at 9pm

CÓRDOBA
Tablao Cardenal
Opposite the Mezquita with a sumptuous 16th-century courtyard setting.
✉ Torrijos 10 ☎ 957 48 33 20 🕐 Tickets: Mon–Sat 11am–10:30pm. Shows: Mon–Sat 10:30pm

GRANADA
Jardines Neptuno
Popular but high-quality flamenco shows.
✉ Calle Arabial ☎ 958 52 25 33 🕐 Daily from 10pm

MÁLAGA
Vista Andalucía
This flamenco show has been castanet-clicking since 1987.
✉ Avenida Los Guindos 29 ☎ 952 23 11 57
🕐 Tue–Sat 10:30pm

MARBELLA
Ana Maria
In the heart of Marbella's old town, this place has a lively bar, with evening flamenco shows, along with other entertainment.

Plaza Santo Cristo 5, Casco Antiquo 952 77 56 46 Summer only

NERJA
El Colonio
Restaurant with performances of flamenco in attractive Andalucian house.
Granada 6 952 52 18 26 Dinner show: summer, Wed–Fri 9:30pm or 10pm; winter, Wed 9pm

RONDA
Circulo de Artistas
Quality flamenco show with plenty of foot-stomping and flouncing frills.
Plaza del Socorro 661 40 31 52 Shows: Mon and Wed 10pm

SEVILLA
El Arenal
Lavish theatre with nightly flamenco.
Calle Rodo 7 954 21 64 92 Shows: 9:30pm and 11:30pm

Los Gallos
Small and intimate; another top show.
Plaza de Santa Cruz 11 954 21 69 81 Shows 9pm and 11:30pm

TORREMOLINOS
Taberna Flamenco Pepe López
Well-known venue for flamenco.
Plaza de la Gamba Alegre 952 38 12 84 Apr to autumn nightly at 10pm

Exploring

The Costa del Sol falls into two parts with Málaga forming the divide between the western and eastern sections. The most developed and best-known area is west of Málaga, starting with Torremolinos and including the major resorts of Benalmádena Costa, Fuengirola, Marbella and Estepona. This part of the coastline is virtually one long stream of apartment blocks, marina developments, hotels and restaurants. The eastern Costa del Sol, stretching towards Almería, has a totally different appeal. Here the coastline is often broken up by rocks and small coves and is much less developed, with Nerja standing out as a favoured resort. The interior offers excursions to white Andalucian villages nestling in the mountains, and to the great cities of Granada, Córdoba and Sevilla.

Málaga

Málaga is the second city of Andalucía and capital of the Costa del Sol. The town is crowned by the old Moorish castle that stands atop the Gibralfaro Hill, holding a commanding view of Málaga's harbour and the wide sweep of the bay.

Málaga

The backing of the Montes de Málaga mountain range provides shelter from the wind, ensuring a pleasant Mediterranean climate, which is particularly agreeable from autumn through to spring. To many tourists Málaga has tended to serve primarily as a gateway to the coast or its hinterland. However, since the opening of the Picasso Museum, along with several other new museums and expansion projects, there is an awakening of interest in the city whose old quarters, churches, traditional bars and restaurants give a true taste of Andalucía.

✚ 20K

LA ALCAZABA

Best places to see, ➤ 36–37.

CASA NATAL DE PICASSO

Spain's celebrated painter Pablo Ruiz Picasso was born in 1881 in the corner house of an elegant yellow-toned block on the Plaza de la Merced. His birthplace was declared an historic-artistic monument in 1983, and in 1991 it became the headquarters of the Pablo Ruiz Picasso Foundation.

The exhibition, covering two floors, includes early sketches by the artist, plus sculptures, photos and family memorabilia.

It was here that Picasso began to paint, helped by his father, an art teacher, who had recognized his young son's talent.

At No 13 on the same plaza, the Foundation has opened an exhibition space for contemporary Spanish painters (same hours as Casa Natal de Picasso).

➕ *Málaga 6a* ✉ Plaza de la Merced 15 ☎ 952 06 02 15 🕐 Mon–Sat 9:30–8:30, Sun 10–2 👆 Inexpensive 🍴 Many nearby (€–€€€) 🚉 Centro-Alameda railway station

CASTILLO DE GIBRALFARO

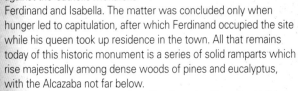

Right above the Alcazaba stands the Castillo de Gibralfaro, crowning the hill of the same name. It was built by Yusef I of Granada at the beginning of the 14th century on a former Phoenician site and lighthouse from which its name was derived – *gebel-faro* (rock of the lighthouse) signifies the beacon that served to guide ships into the harbour.

This was once the scene of a three-month siege by the citizens of Málaga against the Catholic Monarchs Ferdinand and Isabella. The matter was concluded only when hunger led to capitulation, after which Ferdinand occupied the site while his queen took up residence in the town. All that remains today of this historic monument is a series of solid ramparts which rise majestically among dense woods of pines and eucalyptus, with the Alcazaba not far below.

Although it can be reached on foot from the Alcazaba, it's better to get to the castle by bus, car or even horse and carriage. You can round off a visit with a cool drink at the Parador de Málaga, which also offers panoramic views of the harbour and city, with landmarks such as the cathedral and bullring.

➕ *Málaga 7c* ✉ Gibralfaro Mountain ☎ 952 22 72 30 🕐 Daily 9–6 👆 Inexpensive 🍴 *Parador* nearby 🚌 35

a walk

through the Old Town

This walk starts in the Plaza de la Marina and makes a tour of Málaga's old areas, taking in the cathedral and several churches.

From the Plaza de la Marina take Calle Molina Lario, left of the Málaga Palacio Hotel which faces you. A few moments' walk will bring you right up to the cathedral.

Horses and carriages line up here ready to take visitors on a tour around the town. Opposite, on the Plaza Obispo, is the old Palacio Episcopal, which contains some delightful 'hidden' patios and has exhibitions of contemporary art.

Turn right along Calle Santa Maria to take Calle San Agustín.

On your right is the Palacio Buenavista, which now houses the Museo Picasso (➤ 93).

Take a right fork into Calle Granada which takes you by the Iglesia de Santiago. Almost opposite is tiny Tomás de

Cózar 13 leading to Málaga's El Hammam Arab baths. Continue along Calle Granada to the Plaza de la Merced.

The centre of the plaza is marked by an obelisk in memory of General Torrijos and his men who were shot after the War of Independence. On the far corner, in a block of houses, is the Casa Natal de Picasso (➤ 84–85), birthplace of Pablo Picasso, now centre of the Picasso Foundation.

Return down Calle Granada to the Plaza del Siglo and on to the Plaza de la Constitucíon, then stroll down Calle Marqués Larios, Málaga's main shopping street. Down on the left make a short detour through the archway and along Pasaje de Chinitas, which leads to a square. Complete the walk down Calle Larios and turn into the Alameda Principal to the Plaza de la Marina.

Distance 4km (2.5 miles)
Time 3–4 hours, depending on stops
Start/end point Plaza de la Marina 🚇 *Málaga 4c*
Lunch La Posada de Antonio (€€) ✉ Esparteros 4
☎ 952 17 26 29

CATEDRAL

Málaga's cathedral is large and has benefited from being cleaned. It was built between 1528 and 1782 on or near the site of a former mosque. While original plans had allowed for two towers, lack of funds resulted in the completion of only one, giving rise to the name by which the cathedral is affectionately referred to, La Manquita, loosely interpreted as 'the little one-armed woman'. The interior has influences of the Renaissance and baroque styles. The notable 17th-century choir stalls of mahogany and cedarwood were designed by Luis Ortíz. After his death the 40 finely carved statues of the saints behind each stall were completed by Pedro de Mena, one of Spain's most celebrated wood-carvers of the time, who spent some years in Málaga. Some of the chapels leading off the aisles also contain works by Pedro de Mena and his tutor Alonso Cano.

Adjoining the cathedral is the Iglesia del Sagrario. Founded in

the 15th century on the site of a mosque, the church has an unusual rectangular shape. Its Isabelline-Gothic portal is the only remaining part of the original structure, which was rebuilt in 1714. The interior is richly decorated and its main altar features a magnificent 16th-century retable.

✚ *Málaga 5b* ✉ Calle Molina Lario, s/n ☎ 952 21 59 17 🕐 Mon–Sat 10–6 ✋ Inexpensive 🍴 None 🚉 Centro-Alameda railway station

CENTRO (CENTRE)

The heart of Málaga lies north of the Alameda
Principal, Málaga's main avenue, and east of the
Río Guadalmedina, which separates the old town
from the new. As soon as you turn off the Alameda
you enter a labyrinthine medieval world of narrow,
twisting roads. There is much to be enjoyed here,
increasingly so the more you find your bearings.
The centre is compact and many streets are
pedestrian-only, so exploring on foot is both
enjoyable and viable.

Another way in which to enjoy a tour around
town is by horse-drawn carriage, a good option if
you are tired or feeling the heat. You will see these
lined up by the cathedral, in the Paseo del Parque
and various other points around the town.

While the cathedral is a focal point from which
to start exploring, the main artery of the city centre
is the elegant shopping street Calle Marqués de
Larios, which leads from the Alameda Principal
north to the Plaza de la Constitución. On either
side are narrow streets and small squares where
you can happily browse for hours. Within this area
are a number of churches and a few museums,
all within close range. You will also discover
picturesque narrow streets lined with bars, cafés
and both idiosyncratic and sophisticated shops.

Málaga is famed for its *tapas* bars. For some
local atmosphere try one on the so-called *rutas
del tapeo* (*tapas* route) which covers the area west
of Calle Marqués de Larios, centering around
Calle Nueva.

✚ *Málaga 4b* 🍴 Huge choice of restaurants (€–€€€)

CENTRO DE ARTE CONTEMPORÁNEO DE MÁLAGA

CAC Málaga includes contemplative photographic studies and paintings, some of them immense and all given optimum display space. The aim is to pioneer ultramodern artistic trends through four exhibitions: two temporary; one dedicated to up-and-coming Spanish artists; and a changeable, permanent exhibition.

www.cacmalaga.org

✚ *Málaga 2d* ✉ Calle Alemania, s/n ☎ 952 12 00 55 ⓘ Summer Tue–Sun 10–2, 5–9; winter Tue–Sun 10–8 ⛋ Free ⛉ Centro-Alameda railway station

IGLESIA DE LOS MÁRTIRES

The church was founded in 1487 and dedicated to the martyrs of the town. It features a striking Mudéjar tower which was added later and a rich baroque-style interior, with a sculpture by Francisco Ortíz of Jesus praying on the Mount of Olives.

✚ *Málaga 4a* ✉ Plaza Mártires ☎ 952 21 27 24 ⓘ Daily 10–2:30, 6–7:30 ⛋ Free

IGLESIA DE SANTIAGO

Founded in 1490, the church is noted for its tall, Mudéjar-style steeple and baroque interior which contains some notable chapels. Pablo Picasso's baptismal certificate is stored here.

✚ *Málaga 6b* ✉ Calle Granada 62 ☎ 952 21 03 99 ⓘ Daily 9–1:30, 6–9 ⛋ Free

IGLESIA DEL SANTO CRISTO DE LA SALUD

The interior of this 17th-century church is a real gem. Note the brilliant altarpiece and beautifully decorated cupola. The church also contains the tomb of the architect Pedro de la Mena.

✚ *Málaga 4a* ✉ Calle Compañia ☎ 952 21 34 56 ⏱ Daily 9:30–12:30, 6:30–6:30 ✋ Free

IGLESIA SAN JUAN BAUTISTA

Founded in 1490, the church's baroque-style tower above the main entrance was added in 1770. Inside are several fine chapels and a rich altarpiece. The 17th-century figure of San Juan is the work of Francisco Ortíz.

✚ *Málaga 4b* ✉ Calle San Juan 3 ☎ 952 21 12 83 ⏱ Daily 8:30–1, 6–8 (undergoing renovation) ✋ Free

JARDÍN BOTÁNICO 'LA CONCEPCIÓN'

Just outside Málaga, Finca de la Concepción is a magnificent botanical garden. You can follow a marked path through exotic trees and plants, passing Roman sculpture and a waterfall.

✚ *Málaga 5a (off map)*/20J ✉ Along the N331 to Antequera, just off the Málaga ring road ☎ 952 25 21 48 ⏱ Summer Tue–Sun 10–6:30; winter Tue–Sun 10–4 ✋ Inexpensive

MUSEO DE ARTES Y COSTUMBRES POPULARES

This little museum is housed in the Mesón de la Victoria, a former 17th-century inn. The museum provides an insight into the past ways and customs of the people of the region.

Exhibits include a fishing boat and some interiors of old houses, plus displays of costumes, ceramics and tiles, *feria* posters and religious items.

✚ *Málaga 3b* ✉ Pasillo Santa Isabel 10 ☎ 952 21 71 37 ⏱ Summer Mon–Fri 10–1, 5–8, Sat 10–12; rest of year Mon–Fri 10–1, 4–7 ✋ Inexpensive 🚆 Railway station Centro-Alameda

MUSEO CARMEN THYSSEN BORNEMISZA

Open in late 2008, this private collection of 358 works by Spanish artists has been donated by Baroness Thyssen, most famous for the name behind Madrid's, Thyssen-Bornemisza gallery. Housed in a renovated 16th-century palace, the collection includes paintings by Sorolla, Zurbarán and Dominguez Bécquer.

✚ *Málaga 4a* ✉ Calle Compañía, s/n ☎ 952 21 34 45 🕔 Tue–Sun 10–7 ✋ Inexpensive

MUSEO PICASSO

The Picasso Museum is installed in the magnificent Palacio Buenavista. It contains more than 180 works by the artist, including drawings, engravings, lithographs, sculptures and ceramics, the majority of which have been donated by Christina, Picasso's daughter-in-law. There are also temporary exhibitions and displays.

✚ *Málaga 5b* ✉ Palacio de Buenavista, Calle San Agustín 8 ☎ 952 60 27 31 🕔 Tue–Thu 10–8, Fri–Sat 10–9 ✋ Moderate

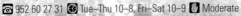

a walk

around the churches & museums of Málaga

This leisurely walk includes Málaga's main market, an attractive small museum and several churches.

From the Alameda Principal cross over at the second traffic lights at the flower market and turn into Calle Torregorda to the Mercado de Atarazas, Malaga's main market.

The market is undergoing renovations but you can still admire the Moorish-style, wrought-iron building fronted by a horseshoe arch. The temporary market is a few blocks down on the corner of Calle Agujero and Paseo Santa Isabel.

Continue right along the Paseo Santa Isabel and you will find yourself on the banks of the dried up Río Guadalmedina. Look for a flight of steps on your right that leads down through a tiny garden to the Museo de Artes y Costumbres Populares (➤ 92). Continue along the Paseo Santa Isabel and turn right down Calle Cisneros.

This brings you into a picturesque part of the old town where a right turn down a narrow alleyway leads to the Iglesia San Juan Bautista (➤ 92), standing on a small square.

Retrace your steps, turn right onto Calle Especerías, left along Calle Salvago, left again and second right to the Plaza San Ignacio.

Take a look at the Iglesia del Corazón de Jesús. Turn back and take the Calle de los Mártires. On the small square that follows you cannot miss the striking Mudéjar tower of the Iglesia de los Mártires (➤ 91).

Return and turn left along Calle Compañia, past the Iglesia de Santo Cristo de la Salud.

Wander through the Plaza de la Constitución and take the Calle Nueva into the heart of the famous area for *tapas* bars. Some refreshments will no doubt be welcome here. The Calle Puerta del Mar leads straight down to the Alameda Principal and back to the station.

Distance 3.5km (2 miles)
Time 3–4 hours, depending on visits
Start/end point Alameda Principal ✚ *Málaga 3c*
Lunch Mesón la Aldea (€) ✉ Esparteros, 5 ☎ 952 22 76 89

PALACIO DE LA ADUANA

The Hall of Columns (Salón de Columnas), in this neoclassical former Customs House, now exhibits parts of the art collection from the Museum of Fine Arts (Museo de Bellas Artes). The exhibitions and displays are changed at regular intervals. Eventually the whole collection will be rehoused in a new Palace of Fine Arts.

➕ *Málaga 5c* ✉ Alcazabilla 2 ☎ 952 21 36 80 🕓 Tue 3–8, Wed–Fri 9–8, Sat–Sun 9–3 ♿ Free 🚉 Centro-Alameda railway station

EL PARQUE

Málaga's city park, which runs alongside the Paseo del Parque, was created at the end of the 19th century on land reclaimed from the sea. The park contains tropical flowering trees and shrubs. Many of the unusual and exotic species were brought from overseas when Málaga was an important trading centre.

➕ *Málaga 5c* ✉ Between Paseo del Parque and Paseo de España ☎ None 🕓 Daily ♿ Free 🚉 Centro-Alameda railway station

SANTUARIO DE LA VICTORIA

The church was erected in 1487 on the site where the Catholic Monarchs pitched their tents during the siege of that year. A major feature is the magnificent retable which rises above the main altar. High up, amid a flourish of exuberant ornamentation, is a small *camerín* (chapel) containing a statue of the Madonna and Child (reached by stairs at the far end of the church). In the crypt is the family vault of the counts of Buenavista, who were responsible for the rebuilding of the church in the 17th century.

➕ *Málaga 8b (off map)* ✉ Plaza del Santuario ☎ 952 25 26 47 🕓 Tue–Fri 10–12, 4:30–7, Sat 10–12 ♿ Free 🚉 Centro-Alameda railway station

HOTELS

Castilla (€)

A solid, no-surprises small hotel near the port with pleasant rooms, some with balconies and the added perk of a parking area. There are plenty of bars and restaurants nearby.

✉ Córdoba 7 ☎ 952 21 86 35

Hotel Atarazanas (€€)

Modern hotel just across from the central market in an elegant building. Rooms are small but comfortable and there is a café and excellent restaurant.

✉ Calle Atarazanas 19 ☎ 952 12 19 10; www.balboahoteles.com

Larios (€€€)

This smart hotel is located on the most fashionable shopping street, a short walk from the cathedral and Málaga's old quarter. Ask for a room overlooking the Plaza de la Constitución.

✉ Calle Marquès de Larios 2 ☎ 952 22 22 00; www.hotel-larios.com

Molino Lario (€€)

The elegant lobby with its grey marble and white leather furnishings reflects the atmosphere throughout with luxurious rooms crowned by a rooftop pool and terrace with cathedral views.

✉ Molino Lario 22 ☎ 952 06 20 02; www.hotelmolinolario.com

Los Naranjos (€€)

A pleasant hotel, on an elegant stretch of street, east of the centre. Rooms on the upper floors have the best sea and coastline views. There are private balconies and good-sized bathrooms, most with a bathtub as well as shower.

✉ Paseo de Sancha 35 ☎ 952 22 43 16; www.hotel-losnaranjos.com

Parador de Málaga – Gibralfaro (€€€)

Surrounded by pine trees on top of Gibralfaro, this grey-stone *parador* has spectacular views of the city and sea. The rooms are rustic and attractive and the restaurant is one of the best in town.

✉ Monte de Gibralfaro ☎ 952 22 19 02; www.parador.es

RESTAURANTS

Adolfo (€€)
Excellent local and international cuisine. The menu includes lobster salad and a variety of vegetarian choices.

✉ Paseo Marítimo Pablo Ruiz Picasso 12 ☎ 952 60 19 14 🕐 Lunch and dinner; closed Sun

Antonio Martín (€€€)
Seafront restaurant specializing in *fritura malagueña* (fried fish).

✉ Playa de la Malagueta ☎ 952 22 73 98 🕐 Lunch and dinner; closed Sun dinner

Café Central (€)
With its tables spilling out onto this pretty square you can start your day with chocolate and *churros* (spiral doughnuts), moving on to the *fino*, *tapas* and traditional dishes later in the day.

✉ Plaza de la Constitución 11 ☎ 952 22 49 72 🕐 All day

Café de Paris (€€€)
The cuisine here has city-slick sophistication with an excellent selection of appertizers, fish and meat.

✉ Calle Vélez Málaga 8 ☎ 952 22 50 43 🕐 Closed Sun and Mon dinner

La Cancela (€)
Two small dining rooms. Specialities include *fritura malagueña* and *ajo blanco* (cold garlic and almond soup).

✉ Calle Denis Belgrano 3 ☎ 952 22 31 25 🕐 Closed Wed dinner

Casa del Guardia (€)
Dating from 1840, this is one of Málaga's oldest bars, lined with barrels. A good place to sample sweet wines and fresh prawns.

✉ Alameda Principal 18 ☎ 952 21 46 80 🕐 Lunch and dinner

El Chinitas (€€)
Known for its good *tapas*. Specializes in Andalucian and Mediterranean dishes.

✉ Calle Moreno Monroy 4–6 ☎ 952 21 09 72 🕐 Lunch and dinner

Citron (€€)

A fashionable new bar and restaurant. Modern artwork adorns the walls and the menu includes contemporary international dishes like cous cous salad and salmon with goat's cheese sauce.

✉ Plaza de la Merced ☎ 952 22 63 99 🕐 Lunch and dinner

Lo Güeno (€)

Typical *tapas* bar offering a choice of more than 75 dishes.

✉ Calle Marín García 9 ☎ 952 22 21 80 🕐 Lunch and dinner

El Legado Celestial (€)

Just round the corner from the train station, this Chinese restaurant has an excellent-value daily buffet that includes spicy tofu, mushrooms and bamboo and chop suey.

✉ Calle Medelin 3 ☎ 952 35 25 21 🕐 Closed Sun

Media Luna (€)

A Moroccan-run restaurant with an earthy, no-frills atmosphere and superb food. Head for one of the outside tables on this buzzing pedestrian street and try the house speciality: cous cous.

✉ Calle Marques 6 ☎ 952 22 59 47 🕐 Lunch and dinner

La Ménsula (€€)

Head here for traditional Andalucian cuisine, in an elegant, yet cosy atmosphere. The menu includes stone-cooked steak, warm fish salad and king prawns with oyster mushrooms.

✉ Calle Trinidad Grund 28 ☎ 952 22 13 14 🕐 Lunch and dinner; closed Sun

Rincón de Mata (€€)

Well known for its excellent *tapas*. Good value all round.

✉ Calle Esparteros 8 ☎ 952 22 31 35 🕐 Lunch and dinner

El Vegetariano de la Alcazabilla (€)

A reliably good vegetarian restaurant near the Roman amphitheatre. There's a very reasonable daily menu, plus extensive a la carte choice including salads, *seitàn* and pasta dishes.

✉ Pozo del Rey 5 ☎ 952 21 48 58 🕐 Closed Sun

SHOPS

CERAMICS
Cerámica Fina
Attractively displayed, well-crafted ceramics of all kinds.
✉ Calle Coronel 5, near the Church of San Juan ☎ 952 22 46 06

FASHION
Mango
One branch of Spain's well-known chain of elegant fashion stores.
✉ Larios 1 ☎ 952 22 31 02

FOOD
Cacao Sampaka
An irresistible chocoholic stop, selling superb chocolates, including spreads, and chocolates laced with tequila, chilli or natural fruits.
✉ Granada 49 ☎ 952 22 33 10

La Mallorquina
This traditional deli is packed with mouthwatering foods, including hams, cheeses, wines and chocolates.
✉ Sagasta 1 ☎ 952 21 33 52

LEATHERWARE
El Caballo
This classy Spanish chain sells quality leatherware, including bags, jackets, belts and briefcases.
✉ Antonio Díaz 7 ☎ 952 22 20 39

DEPARTMENT STORES
El Corte Inglés
Six floors of fashion, gifts and exhibitions of arts and crafts.
✉ Avenida de Andalucia 4–6 ☎ 952 30 00 00

Vialia Centro Comercial
New shopping centre with international and Spanish high-street names, including Hennes, Botticelli, Zara Home and Sfera.
✉ Adjacent to new Renfe station

ENTERTAINMENT

CINEMA AND THEATRE

Albéniz Multicines

Large municipal cinema showing current releases, as well as international films with original sound tracks.

⊠ Alcazabilla 4 ☎ 952 21 58 98

Teatro Miguel de Cervantes

An excellent programme of concerts, dance and theatre.

⊠ Ramos Martín, s/n ☎ 952 22 41 00; www.teatrocervantes.com

Yelmo Cineplex

Original-version films.

⊠ Avenida Alfonso Ponce Léon, Plaza Mayor ☎ 902 20 21 03

CLUBS

Liceo

Attracts a local student crowd with its thumping music.

⊠ Calle Beatas 21 ☎ No phone

Warhol

Gay clubbers enjoy the funky mix of house and rock here.

⊠ Calle Niño de Guevara, s/n ☎ No phone

ZZ Club

Popular with students. Live music, including rock on Thursdays.

⊠ Calle Téjon y Rodriguez 6 ☎ No phone

SPORT

These two clubs near Málaga offer hang-gliding and paragliding courses for beginners, and tandem flights with an instructor.

Club Escuela Parapente el Valle

⊠ Calle Sevilla 4, Valle de Abdalajís ☎ 952 48 91 80

Club Vuelo Libre Málaga

⊠ Calle Sevilla 2, Valle de Abdalajís ☎ 952 48 92 98

West of Málaga

This is the most popular part of the Costa del Sol, which attracts mass tourism to the crowded and lively resorts of Torremolinos and Fuengirola. But this long ribbon of holiday development, backed by wonderful mountain scenery, has lots more to offer.

Fashionable haunts such as Puerto Banús and Marbella have an upmarket image and offer excitement and glamour. Smaller, typically Spanish towns, such as San Roque and San Pedro de Alcántara, provide the chance to relax in the shade of a pretty plaza. Or you can seek out solitude in one of the remote clifftop villages and towns scattered across the peaks and valleys inland from the coast. The modern city of Sevilla, the capital of Andalucía, has an abundance of culture and fine architecture as well as great shopping opportunities. The diversity, plus wonderful sandy beaches and almost year-long sunshine, is what makes this stretch of coastline so alluring and why visitors return again and again.

ANTEQUERA

Antequera is known for its convents, 30-plus churches and elegant mansions. It is easily reached by means of the good motorway from Málaga and can be visited in a day (town walk ➤ 106–107 and drive from Torremolinos ➤ 138–139).

The town is dominated by the old castle, which has excellent views of the surrounding plains. The 16th-century Church of Santa María la Mayor, nearby, features a fine Mudéjar ceiling. Dominant are the bell towers of the churches of San Sebastian and San Augustín, which combine the Mudéjar and baroque styles. Outstanding is the Church of El Carmen, which has been designated a national monument. Formerly a convent, it is noted for its rich interior and impressive wooden altar.

The discovery of prehistoric tombs in nearby caves has given the town added importance. Of the three caves here, the most important is the **Dólmen de Menga.** Its large cavern contains a series of stones and columns which support huge slabs that form the roof, believed to date back to *c*2500 BC.

The Parque Nacional Torcal de Antequera is some 16km (10 miles) south of Antequera and covers an extended area of grey limestone rocks and boulders, weathered with time to form the most weird and wonderful shapes. There is a large new information centre by the parking area and a magnificent view from the nearby Mirador el Ventanillo. Walking trails are marked by arrows (green for a shorter walk, yellow for a longer one).

www.antequera.es

✚ 20J ✉ 54km (33.5 miles) north of Málaga 🍴 Good choice of restaurants (€–€€€) 🚌 From Málaga 🚆 From Málaga ❓ Fería de Primavera (31 May–1/2 Jun); Noche Flamenca de Santa Maria (end Jul); August Fair (early Aug) ℹ Plaza San Sebastian 7 ☎ 952 70 25 05

Dólmen de Menga

✉ 1km (0.6 miles) east of Antequera 🕐 Wed–Sat 9–6, Tue, Sun 9–3:30 ✋ Free 🚌 From Antequera 🚆 From Antequera

BENALMÁDENA COSTA

Benalmádena Costa is a natural extension of Torremolinos, taking over where Torremolinos leaves off. It covers a long stretch of coast lined with the type of high-rise apartment blocks that characterize this section of the Costa del Sol, along with a string of restaurants, cafés, bars and shops. An attractive seafront promenade makes it possible to walk from Torremolinos all the way along the coast to Benalmádena's Puerto Deportivo (➤ 109) – you need time and energy for this!

The area has been noticeably upgraded, partly due to the Casino and the 18-hole Torrequebrada golf course, a short distance up into the hills. There are also facilities for waterskiing, jetskiing, windsurfing, sailing and all the popular water sports.

www.benalmadena.com

✚ 20L ✉ 20km (12 miles) west of Málaga 🍴 Numerous restaurants and bars (€–€€€) 🚌 Connections 🚆 Railway station Benalmádena–Arroyo de la Miel ❓ Virgen del Carmen fiesta (16 Jul) ℹ Avenida Antonio Machado 10 ☎ 952 44 12 95

a walk around Antequera's churches and mansions

This walk takes in some of Antequera's many churches and includes magnificent views. Most churches close from 1.30 to 4pm so a morning walk is recommended. On the Plaza San Sebastian look at the 16th-century Colegiata de San Sebastian. Walk up Calle Infante Don Fernando. Take a look at the Iglesia de San Agustín, on the left, and farther along, on the right, you will pass the Palacio Consistorial (Town Hall) and the Convento de los Remedios.

Just past the Iglesia de San Juan de Dios turn sharp right into Calle Cantareros and back towards the centre.

You will pass the house of the Condado de Colchado and the Convento de la Madre de Dios de Monteagudo.

Continue down Calle Diego Ponce, then turn left up to Plaza San Francisco and the Plazuela de San Zoilo.

This brings you to the Convento Real de San Zoilo, one of Antequera's National Monuments, and some fine views.

Take Calle Calzada and continue up Cuesta de Los Rojos to Plaza del Carmen. On Calle del Carmen is the Iglesia del Carmen. Return and take a sharp right, turn up Calle del Colegio, a very steep climb, to the Arco de los Gigantes (Arch of Giants) on your left. There are stunning panoramic views from the mirador here.

Pass through the arch to the Real Colegiata de Santa Maria la Mayor. Nearby are the Roman Baths.

Return through the arch and go left along Calle Herradores to the charming Plaza del Portichuelo and the Iglesia de Santa Maria de Jesús.

Distance 4.5km (3 miles)
Time About 3 hours
Start point Plaza San Sebastian
End point Plaza del Portichuelo
Lunch Restaurante El Angelote
(€€) ✉ Plaza Coso Viejo
☎ 952 70 34 65

BENALMÁDENA PUEBLO

Two small inland communities present a complete contrast to the attractions on the coastal strip of Benalmádena Costa. About 1km (0.6 miles) into the hills is Arroyo de la Miel which has developed into a lively centre with modern housing, shops and restaurants. Just up the road is the Tivoli World amusement park.

Farther up the hill is Benalmádena Pueblo, whose origins are thought to date back to Phoenician times. This is a charming village of narrow twisting streets and whitewashed houses. With attractive views of the coast and surrounding landscapes, it offers a rural atmosphere. The Museo Arqueológico contains some pre-Columbian exhibits, along with objects from Roman and early Iberian times.

✚ 19L ✉ 3km (2 miles) west of Arroyo de la Miel 🍴 Variety of restaurants and bars ❓ Local fair (15 Aug); Fería de San Juan (24 Jun) at Arroyo de la Miel

BENALMÁDENA PUERTO MARINA

Benalmádena's Puerto Marina, or Puerto Deportivo as it is known, has developed into one of the most prominent of the marinas that have sprung up along the coast.

Built initially as a small harbour surrounded by a ring of whitewashed houses, Andalucian-style, it has gradually grown into an impressive marina, with more than 1,000 berths. Numerous shops, open-air bars and restaurants line the quayside. A centrepiece is provided by a complex of luxurious apartments called Las Islas de Puerto Marina. Constructed in flamboyant style,

they do appear like islands floating on the water.

The marina makes a good outing for all age groups. An outstanding attraction is Sea Life Benalmádena, which can be enjoyed by the whole family. You can also catch a ferry from here to Fuengirola (Tue and Sun 10:30, 12:30, 2:30) and enjoy the coastline from the sea.

With its open-air cafés, restaurants and shops, Puerto Marina continues to increase in popularity, especially at weekends, attracting Spaniards and visitors alike with further expansion planned. An ultra-modern underwater lighting system, installed in the waters of the harbour, creates a magical effect at night.

✚ 20L ✉ Benalmádena Costa 🍴 Variety of restaurants, bars and pubs

CASARES

Best places to see, ➤ 40–41.

CÓRDOBA

Córdoba is one of Andalucía's richest jewels. In addition to the
Mezquita or Great Mosque (▶ 48–49), the city's old quarter of
narrow streets with flower-filled balconies and patios allows
visitors an insight into the essence of southern Spain. The town
lies along the banks of the River Guadalquivir, overlooked by the
Sierra de Córdoba. With extremes of heat in the summer and
harsh winters, a good time to visit is spring or autumn.

Tools found on the banks of the River Guadalquivir suggest that
palaeolithic man lived here. Córdoba later became a leading centre
of the people of Tartessos and was then conquered by the
Carthaginians, the Romans (when it became the capital of Baetica)
and the Moors.

In 929, under Moorish rule, the Caliphate of Córdoba
was established. With the founding of a university,
Córdoba became a renowned hub of art, culture and
learning. This period saw the construction of Córdoba's
great Mezquita and other fine examples of Moorish
architecture.

Gradually, in the 11th and 12th centuries, Córdoba went
into decline. With the breaking up of the Caliphate into
small *tarifas* (states), Córdoba came under the jurisdiction
of Sevilla. After it fell to the Christians in 1236, the Catholic
Monarchs presided here while planning the reconquest of
Granada and it was here that Queen Isabella granted
Columbus the commission for his voyage of discovery.

The city has many attractions and should be explored on
foot. Bear in mind that some of its narrow streets do not
easily accommodate pedestrians and cars simultaneously!
The Judería (old Jewish Quarter) is a delightful area of
narrow cobbled streets and white houses. Brilliantly
coloured flowers adorn small squares and beautiful ornate
patios can be seen through doorways.

www.turiscordoba.es

🚹 9B ✉ 187km (116 miles) north of Málaga 🍴 Choice of restaurants (€–€€€) 🚌 Estación de Autobuses, Plaza de las Tres Culturas ☎ 957 40 40 40 🚆 Estación de RENFE, Avenida de América ☎ 902 24 02 02 ❓ Córdoba Patios competition (May), Easter ceremonies; Fair (May); International Festival of Music, Theatre and Dance (Aug); National Festival of Folklore (Sep) ℹ Calle Torrijos 10 ☎ 957 47 12 35

Alcázar de los Reyes Cristianos

This Mudéjar-style palace was begun by King Alfonso XI in the early 14th century. Outstanding Roman mosaics, the old Moorish courtyard and baths still remain. This was once the residence of the Catholic Monarchs, and a one-time Moorish prison.

✉ Campo Santo de los Mártires ☎ 957 42 01 51 🕐 Tue–Sat 10–2, 4:30–6:30; Sun 9:30–2:30 ✋ Inexpensive; free Fri

La Mezquita

Best places to see, ➤ 48–49.

Museo Arqueológico

Housed in the attractive 16th-century Palacio de los Páez, the museum has a fine collection of objects from prehistoric to Roman and Moorish times.

✉ Plaza Jerónimo Páez 7 ☎ 957 35 55 17 🕓 Wed–Sat 9–8:30, Tue 2:30–8:30, Sun 9–2:30 ✋ Inexpensive; free to EU citizens

Museo de Bellas Artes

This fine arts museum contains paintings and sculptures by some of Spain's great masters including Goya, Luis Maroles and Alonso.

✉ Plaza de Potro 1 ☎ 957 35 55 50 🕓 Wed–Sat 9–8:30, Tue 2:30–8:30, Sun 9–2:30 ✋ Inexpensive; free to EU citizens

Museo Municipal Taurino

The Municipal Bullfighting Museum, which is housed in an elegant 16th-century mansion, has an unusual and fascinating display of items and memorabilia relating to some of Córdoba's most famous bullfighters, including the legendary Manolete.

✉ Plaza Maimónides 5 ☎ 957 20 10 56
🕐 Tue–Sat 10–2, 4:30–6:30, Sun and public hols 9:30–2:30 ✋ Inexpensive; free Fri

Palacio de Viana

The Viana Palace warrants a visit, if only to see the beautiful patios and gardens of this fine 15th-century building. There are collections of paintings, porcelain, furniture and tapestries worth seeing. Note the splendid Mudéjar ceiling above the stairway to the first floor. Visitors are given a one-hour guided tour.

✉ Plaza de Don Gome 2 ☎ 957 49 67 41 🕐 Oct–May Mon–Fri 10–1, 4–6, Sat 10–1; mid-Jun to Sep 9–2; closed 1–15 Jun, Sun, public hols ✋ Inexpensive

Torre de La Calahorra

Housed in the 14th-century Moorish fortress across the river, the Museo Histórico (Córdoba City Museum) makes clever use of multi-vision presentations to trace the history of Córdoba at the height of its golden era.

✉ Puente Romano ☎ 957 29 39 29
🕐 Daily 10–6 ✋ Inexpensive

ESTEPONA

Some 36km (22 miles) west of Marbella is Estepona, another of the Costa del Sol's fast-developing resorts. It offers the attractions of a long beach, pleasant seafront promenade, a marina and at least three golf courses. It is also a good base for sailing and windsurfing. This former fishing village retains a large fleet protected by a harbour which also has moorings for some 400 yachts and pleasure craft. An enjoyable pastime is to wander down to the port early in the morning and watch the fresh catch being sold at the fish market.

The old town dates back to Roman and Moorish times. The focal point is the charming little square of the Plaza de las Flores, entered by four archways of trees. Amid trim orange trees and tropical plants, this is a good place in which to linger over a drink. The surrounding area offers a pleasant stroll through narrow streets lined with picturesque houses. Take a look at the Moorish tower on Plaza de la Roloj and go down the steps to the Mercado Municipal, a covered market for fruit, vegetables and fresh fish. Above the little town are old castle ruins.

www.estepona.es

✛ 17L ✉ 82km (51 miles) west of Málaga 🍴 Many restaurants and bars (€–€€€) ❓ Fiesta de San Isidro (15 May); local festival (early Jul); Fiesta de Virgen del Carmen (16 Jul)

ℹ Avenida San Lorenzo 1 ☎ 952 80 20 02

FUENGIROLA

Some 9km (5.5 miles) west of Benalmádena Costa is the prominent resort of Fuengirola, once a peaceful little fishing village. Now the scene is one of solid high-rise apartment blocks and buildings. The old part of the town, however, presents another side of Fuengirola. A lively meeting place is the Plaza de la Constitución, which is dominated by Fuengirola's main church. Southwest of the town is the old Moorish Castle, Castillo de Sohail. The castle, which is thought to have originated with the Romans, was rebuilt by the Moors and destroyed in the 15th century during the Christian reconquest. The present structure dates from 1730 and is open to the public, as well as being a summer venue for concerts. A walk up here is recommended for the excellent coastal views.

Fuengirola is popular with northern Europeans who come for extended stays in the winter. There are many English-run bars and souvenir shops here and in the former fishermen's district of neighbouring Los Boliches. The summer season is always lively; the long sweep of beach appeals to families. Fuengirola has several other attractions geared to children, such as the excellent zoo, an Aquapark at nearby Mijas Costa and the ever-popular Tivoli World up the road.

Water sports are on offer and the resort has an attractive yacht club and marina, along with an extended promenade, the Paseo Marítimo linking Fuengirola, Los Boliches, and Carvajal, which has so far retained a more Spanish feel and has a lovely beach.

www.fuengirola.org

🚌 19L 🖂 29km (18 miles) west of Málaga 🍴 Many restaurants (€–€€€) 🚏 Corner Avenida Ramón y Cajal and Calle Alfonso XIII 🚉 RENFE station at Avenida Jesús Santos Rein (half-hourly service to Málaga via the airport) ℹ Paseo Jesús Santos Rein 6 ☎ 952 46 74 57

GAUCÍN

About 40 minutes away from the coast between Casares and Ronda, Gaucín is yet another of those enchanting little white towns you come across while travelling around the Andalucian countryside. As you approach you will encounter a cluster of whitewashed houses, topped by red roofs, spread out beneath the rocks.

The old Moorish fortress, Castillo de Aguila (Eagle's Castle), now partly restored, stands high above the village, forming a silhouette against the backdrop of mountains. From this vantage point there are magnificent views across the valley of the Guadiaro River, reaching out to the coastline as far as the Rock of Gibraltar.

The village is delightful and is filled with flowers and plants. Its narrow streets and one-way system are not conducive to driving,

however, and the place is best explored on foot. The daily fish market is always a lively event.

Gaucín makes a good base from which to explore the hinterland, which is dotted with attractive towns and villages such as Ronda, Grazalema, Casares, Ubrique and Jimena de la Frontera.

🕂 17K ✉ 120km (75 miles) west of Málaga 🍴 Several restaurants 🚌 Local bus services ❓ Romería San Juan (23 Jun); Fería Virgen de las Nieves (second week Aug); Fiesta de Santo Niño (8, 9 and 10 Sep) ℹ️ Calle Fuente 91, Casares ☎ 952 89 41 26

LA GIRALDA Y LA CATEDRAL, SEVILLA

Best places to see, ➤ 46–47.

GIBRALTAR

The Rock, as it is commonly known, is a popular day trip from the Costa del Sol and is increasingly developing into a fascinating destination in its own right, with recent planned projects including an oceanfront development with casino and luxury apartments, restaurants and shops, a new airport terminal, developing the beaches and continuing to promote Gibraltar's extraordinary history which has resulted in the current anomaly of cultures and religions; the latter including Jews, Muslims, Catholics, Christians and Mormons.

Gibraltar is very much like Britain, with double-decker buses, red post boxes, British-uniformed police and familiar shopping chains like BHS, Dorothy Perkins, Top Shop and Marks & Spencer.

There are plenty of sights that help illustrate a history that stretches back to prehistoric times; a Neanderthal skull was discovered in one of the rock's numerous caves in 1848, a reproduction of which can be seen in the Gibraltar Museum.

www.gibraltar.gov.gi

➕ 16M ✉ 78km (48 miles) southwest of Marbella 🍴 Choice of restaurants (€–€€€)

ℹ Duke of Kent House, Cathedral Square ☎ 200 74 950

Europa Point

One of the two ancient pillars of Hercules, this is the perfect viewing point for gazing across the straits to Morocco. The lighthouse here dates from 1841 and marks the meeting place of the Atlantic and the Mediterranean.

Gibraltar Museum

This fascinating museum has displays including a Hackney carriage, Phoenician pots and bowls, Lord Nelson's shoe buckle, marine and mammal exhibits, and a cast of the Neanderthal skull discovered in Forbes Quarry. It also houses a beautifully restored 14th-century Moorish bathhouse

✉ Bomb House Lane ☎ 200 74 289 🕐 Mon–Sat 10–6, Sat 10–2
🖐 Inexpensive

Trafalgar Cemetery

Evocative, overgrown Trafalgar Cemetery includes graves of the British sailors who were killed at the Battle of Trafalgar, with their touching tombstone inscriptions. ✉ Prince Edward's Road 🕐 Daily 9–6

The Upper Rock Reserve

Entry to this natural reserve includes St Michael's Cave, the Apes' Den and the Great Siege Tunnels. St Michael's Cave is also a performing arts venue and is stunning with its large cavern spaces hung with stalactites and stalagmites. The Barbary apes are not shy of tourists, but should not

be handled (or fed) as they can bite. The Siege Tunnels were carved out during the Great Siege of 1779 and form part of one of the most impressive defence systems in the world.

🕐 Daily 9:30–7 🖐 Moderate

MARBELLA

Marbella is synonymous with the hedonistic world of the jet set. Since its meteoric rise to fame, Marbella has indeed never ceased to set itself above its fellow resorts along the coast, by continuing to cultivate its image as a playground of the rich and famous with their luxury yachts and glamorous life-styles.

Marbella's development can be traced back to the 1940s, with the founding of the El Rodeo restaurant and inn by the Spanish aristocrat Ricardo Soriano. His nephew, Prince Alfonso Hohenlohe of Liechtenstein, went on to develop a small beach property into the Marbella Club complex for his friends among the international set. This continued to attract celebrities to the area and led to the construction of a string of luxurious hotels which were built along the coast on either side of Marbella town, offering beautiful gardens, pools and sports facilities.

After the halcyon days of the 1970s and early '80s, there was an economic slump. Marbella went into a decline and began to wane in popularity. Then in the early 1990s, ambitious programmes were put forward to give the resort a much needed facelift. The remodelling of the Paseo Marítimo, the planting of palms and beautifying of the beaches, along with the construction of sorely needed underground parking areas and pledges to clean the place up in general, did much to restore Marbella's image and prestige. Marbella continues to prosper and grow. Urban developments spread out in all directions, while more projects are underway to propagate the image of the 'New Marbella'.

There are several Marbellas – the town itself, now a busy commercial hub, the beachfront and marina, and its picturesque old quarter, the Casco Antiguo (Old Town) (► 42–43). In the heart of Marbella town there are plush apartments overlooking the sea. From the Casco Antiguo a short walk will take you to the Parque de la Alameda (Alameda Park). The pleasant little park features exotic plants, trees and fountains, with attractively tiled benches adding to the scene. Stroll down to the beachfront through the Avenida del Mar, a broad pedestrian-only avenue adorned with flowers and trees and a series of lively Salvador Dalí sculptures.

The Paseo Marítimo, which stretches far on either side of town, offers an enjoyable seafront stroll, with bars and restaurants lining the route. Many improvements have been made to the long stretch of beach, shaded at regular intervals by palm trees. Have

a wander around the Puerto Deportivo (yacht harbour), where you can linger over a drink or a meal.

Two museums (in and around the Old Town) are worth a visit; the **Museo Bonsai,** for its delightful collection of Japanese-style minature trees, and the **Museo del Grabado Español Contemporáneo** (Museum of Spanish Contemporary Prints), for its exhibitions, which include works by prominent Spanish artists.

The municipality of Marbella covers a 28km (17-mile) stretch of coastline, which extends from the marina and the residential area of Cabo Pino, east of the town, to Guadalmina out to the west. The section from Marbella to Guadalmina has come to be known as the Golden Mile, so named for the concentration of luxurious hotels, restaurants and golf courses to be found here. Expensive villas with pools, set amid gardens of lush, tropical vegetation, complete the picture.

References to the 'exclusive resort of Marbella' can be misleading as, more often than not, the term applies not to the town, but to the hotels strung out on either side, including the plush Guadalmina development and the Puerto Banús

marina. This area is, in effect, the 'playground' of the jet set.

Puerto Banús (➤ 54–55) is officially part of San Pedro de Alcántara (➤ 128–129, located 3km/2 miles away) and is usually listed under Nueva Andalucía. However, it is within the community of Marbella and tends to be included in references to the town. It continues to be a place of pure enjoyment and a magnet for yachties. The marina has berths for over 900 and attracts craft of all sizes; millionaires' yachts are a common sight. There are also facilities for many water sports.

Marbella continues to attract the celebrities and stars. The partying goes on but has become less visible as more of the social scene takes place privately.

www.marbella.es

✚ 18L ✉ 56km (35 miles) west of Málaga 🍴 Wide range of restaurants (€–€€€) 🚌 Bus station, Avenida del Trapiche, s/n ☎ 952 76 44 00. Avenida Ricardo Soriano for local services ❓ Carnival (pre-Lent), Fería de la Vírgen del Carmen (16 Jul), Fería de San Bernabé Patrón (Jun), Fería de San Pedro (Oct) ❗ Glorieta de la Fontanilla, Paseo Marítimo ☎ 952 77 14 42; Plaza de los Naranjos ☎ 952 82 35 50

Arco de Marbello
✉ CN-340, Km183.5 ☎ 952 82 28 18

Museo Bonsai
✉ Parque Arroyo de la Represa ☎ 952 86 29 26 🕐 Daily 10–1:30, 4:30–8 🚌 Avenida Ricardo Soriano 💶 Inexpensive

Museo del Grabado Español Contemporáneo
✉ Hospital Bazán, s/n ☎ 952 76 57 41 🕐 Mon–Fri 10–2, 5:30–8:30, Sun 10–2 🚌 Avenida Ricardo Soriano 💶 Inexpensive

MARBELLA'S CASCO ANTIGUO
Best places to see, ➤ 42–43.

LA MEZQUITA, CÓRDOBA
Best places to see, ➤ 48–49.

MIJAS
Best places to see, ➤ 50–51.

PUERTO BANÚS
Best places to see, ➤ 54–55.

RONDA
Ronda is renowned for its spectacular setting. The views of the ravine and surrounding landscapes, its historical background and legends of bandits, all add to a certain mystique, which continues to attract visitors. A mighty split in the El Tajo gorge, spanned by the Puente Nuevo (➤ 52–53), divides the town into Old Ronda (La Ciudad) and the newer part, known as El Mercadillo.

Most monuments of note are in the old town, which retains Moorish influences. These include the imposing Church of Santa Maria la Mayor, the Minaret of San Sebastian, the Palacio de Mondragón and the Casa del Gigante, the Palacio del Marqués de Salvatierra and the gardens of the Casa del Rey Moro. The Museo Lara (Science and History) and Museo del Bandolero (History and Legends of local bandits) are also worth a visit. The café-lined Plaza del Socorro is the focal point of the newer part of town, Ronda's main shopping centre, with more magnificent views from the attractive gardens of the Alameda del Tajo nearby.

Ronda has long-standing associations with bullfighting. The bullring, near the Puente Nuevo, was built in 1785 and is Spain's oldest. It was here that the rules of modern bullfighting were laid down by Francisco Romero, whose grandson Pedro Romero became one of Spain's most famous matadors. The bullring, now owned by Antonio Ordoñez, another of the greats, is used only for special fiestas. The bullfighting museum behind the ring contains glittering costumes, gear and photographs.

Ronda is a city with a romantic past. Two famous Americans, writer Ernest Hemingway and actor Orson Welles, were keen followers of the bullfight. Both spent much time here and each of them formed a close friendship with Ordoñez. By his request, Welles' ashes are scattered over the bullfighter's nearby ranch.

Some 20km (12.5 miles) southwest of Ronda is the **Cueva de la Pileta** (Pileta Cave), which has significant prehistoric rock paintings of animals, outlined in black and red, believed to date back more than 25,000 years.

www.turismoderonda.es

🕂 17J ✉ 118km (73 miles) northwest of Málaga 🍴 Many restaurants (€–€€€) 🚌 Buses from Algeciras, Málaga (via Bobadilla) ❓ Pedro Romero Festival (➤ 25)

ℹ Plaza de España 1 ☎ 952 18 71 19

Cueva de la Pileta

✉ 20km (12.5 miles) southwest of Ronda ☎ 952 16 73 43 🕐 Daily 10–1, 4–6; tours last about one hour ✋ Inexpensive

a walk in and around Ronda

This walk starts in the Plaza de España and takes you across the bridge to explore the old town of Ronda.

From the Plaza de España walk towards the Puente Nuevo (New Bridge).

Take a walk around the *parador*, on your right, for spectacular views of the gorge.

Return and cross over the bridge.

Look down into the ravine as you pass. A right turn down

Calle Tenorio will take you into a network of narrow streets and neat white houses to the Plaza del Campillo.

Keep walking and at the far end look for steps leading down the hill.

A short walk down reveals Ronda's houses perched on the clifftop. A further walk down will provide you with the classic view of the bridge, but it's a long climb up!

Head back up again and take the small street ahead to the Plaza Mondragón.

On the right is the Palacio de Mondragón, which was once a Moorish palace.

Continue to Plaza de la Duquesa de Parcent. A left turn leads to the entrance of the Colegiata de Santa María la Mayor. Take the short slope down to Calle Armiñan and turn left. Note the Minaret of San Sebastian before crossing over to turn sharp right.

There are fine carvings on the facade of the Palacio del Marqués de Salvatierra (closed to the public).

Climb up Calle Santo Domingo to the Casa del Rey Moro, where you can take a long winding staircase down to the river and back up again to the gardens. Rejoin Calle Armiñán and cross back over the bridge to the Plaza de España.

Distance 4km (2.5 miles)
Time 2–3 hours
Start/end point Plaza de España
Lunch Pedro Romero (€€) ✉ Virgen de la Paz 18, Ronda
☎ 952 87 11 10

RONDA'S PUENTE NUEVO

Best places to see, ➤ 52–53.

SAN PEDRO DE ALCÁNTARA

San Pedro de Alcántara has undergone a facelift in recent years, with pleasing results. A development programme incorporating a new coastal promenade and beach improvements, stretching from Puerto Banús to Guadalmina, has given it a boost as an increasingly popular resort.

On the northern side of the coastal road is the small town itself, which has a neat, pleasant appearance. The Calle Marqués del Duero, attractively shaded by orange trees and palms, and lined with shops and cafés, leads up the hill to the small square of Plaza de la Iglesia adorned by a fountain. Adjacent to the town hall is San Pedro's parish church. Its white facade framed by two palm trees makes an attractive picture.

San Pedro is the first centre in Spain to have introduced the sport of cable skiing, which involves the water skier being towed by cable for long distances.

Three archaeological sites in the vicinity are worth exploring: the

sixth-century Visigoth
Basílica de Vega del
Mar, the Villa Romana
de Río Verde, remnants
of a Roman villa from
the first century, and
Las Bovedas, where the
remains of old Roman
thermal baths can
be seen.

✠ 18L ✉ 70km (43 miles)
west of Málaga 🍴 Choice
of restaurants and bars
(€–€€€)
ℹ Avenida Marques del
Duero 69 ☎ 952 78 52 52

SAN ROQUE/SOTOGRANDE

This is the place for big-time golfers and is said
to have Spain's highest proportion of registered
golfers in any one centre. Among the four golf
courses, the Valderrama Robert Trent Jones Course
played host to the 1997 Ryder Cup. Polo is also played
here during the summer and the Sotogrande Marina
is another attraction.

The small town is an attractive base in itself with
narrow streets and plenty of flowers and plants. The
lively cafés and restaurants of the Campamento area
appeal to a younger crowd.

✠ 16L ✉ 100km (62 miles) west of Málaga 🍴 Wide choice
🚌 Bus connections ❓ San Roque Annual Fair
(early Sep); Sotogrande golf tournaments, polo matches
(Jul, Aug, Sep)
ℹ Avenida 20 Abril, s/n, La Línea ☎ 956 76 99 50

around Andalucian towns and villages

This drive takes you into the rugged landscape of the Serranía de Ronda and through several of the region's most attractive mountain towns.

From the east side of San Pedro de Alcántara, take the turning to Ronda (➤ 124–125).

The A376 (Ruta de la Serranía de Ronda) is fairly wide and has a good surface as it twists its way up into the mountains, offering fine views. The route takes you through pine forests, rocks and white cliffs, until Ronda comes into view, about an hour later (50km/31 miles). Allow time to visit Ronda and have some lunch at the Don Miguel restaurant which offers a dramatic view of the steep cliff on which the town is built.

Return through the old town and take the A369, in the direction of Algeciras, to Gaucín (➤ 116–117).

This section passes through barren hills and rocks and wide open vistas, and includes a bad stretch of road. Take a look at the white hillside town of Gaucín.

Join the A377, direction Manilva-Algeciras. Some 16km (10 miles) on take a sharp left turn to the photogenic town of Casares (➤ 40–41).

The road leads shortly to a stunning view of this white Andalucian town sprawled over the hillside. Continue towards the town and take a left fork uphill for an even more spectacular sight of the town, crowned by the old fortress.

Follow the signs to Estepona and take the old road, which winds down through fertile country to the coast. You should reach Estepona (▶ 114) some 25 minutes later. Rejoin the A7 and head east back to San Pedro.

Distance 145km (90 miles)
Time About 8 hours
Start/end point San Pedro de Alcántara ✚ 18L
Lunch Hotel-Restaurante Don Miguel, Ronda (€€) ✉ Villanueva 4 y 8, Ronda ☎ 952 87 10 90

SEVILLA

Sevilla is the capital of Andalucía and Spain's fourth largest city. It is dominated by La Giralda and the great cathedral that this minaret tower adjoins (▶ 46–47). Various cultures have left their mark here, from the Romans to the Moors and the Christians. An early carving on the Jerez Gate alludes to the legendary origins of the city: 'Hercules built me, Caesar surrounded me with walls and towers, the King Saint took me.'

Sevilla is believed to have been founded by the Iberians. Subsequent occupiers included the Greeks, Phoenicians and the Carthaginians (who named it Hispalis). Around 205BC the town was taken over by the Romans and it continued to flourish under Julius Caesar. During the fifth century it became the capital of the Visigoths. It was captured in AD712 by the Moors, whose long occupation has left magnificent traces of their artistic merits.

In 1248 Sevilla was reconquered by Ferdinand III of Castille. But it was the discovery of America that brought prosperity to Sevilla, when Columbus returned here from his first voyage in 1493. In the 16th and 17th centuries the port became the most important in Spain. During this period, the Sevilla school of painters brought great prestige to the city.

Sevilla is a city to explore on foot with the cathedral a good focal point from which to start. The medieval quarter of the Barrio Santa Cruz is a delightful maze of narrow streets and whitewashed houses adorned with wrought-iron balconies decked with flowers.

A stroll around town reveals mansions, squares and lovely parks, such as the Parque de Maria Luisa, the Murillo gardens and those of the Reales Alcazares. The large Plaza de España contains a tiny canal, decorated bridges and fountains. Over the bridge is the former gypsy Triana area. Alternative ways of getting around are by 'SevillaTour' buses or in a horse-drawn carriage.

www.turismosevilla.org

✚ 3C ✉ 219km (136 miles) northwest of Málaga 🍴 Restaurants and *tapas* bars 🚌 Bus stations: Prado de San Sebastián ☎ 954 41 71 11; Plaza de Armas ☎ 954 90 77 37 🚊 Estación de FFCC Santa Justa, Avenida Kansas City, s/n ☎ 954 54 02 02 🎉 Semana Santa (Easter), Feria de Sevilla (two weeks after Easter), Corpus Christi, Fiesta de la Virgen de los Reyes (15 Aug) ℹ Avenida de la Constitucíon 21B ☎ 954 22 14 04

Casa de Pilatos

This 16th-century private mansion is one of Sevilla's jewels. Combining Mudéjar, Gothic and Renaissance styles, its patios, archways and salons are adorned with delicate carving, tilework and wooden coffered ceilings. A grand staircase leads to the upper floors, which contain a collection of art. The adjoining gardens may also be visited.

✉ Plaza Pilatos 1 ☎ 954 22 52 98 🕐 Daily 9–6 🚌 C1, C2, C3, C4 👆 Moderate; free Tue pm

Museo Arqueológico

Housed in the Renaissance palace built for the 1929 Ibero-America Exhibition, the Archaeological Museum has a fine collection of objects from prehistory and the Moorish culture. Outstanding among its exhibits is the Carombolo Treasure; dating from the seventh century, this includes jewellery from the Tartessos civilization.

✉ Plaza de América ☎ 954 23 24 01 🕐 Wed–Sat 9–8, Tue 3–8, Sun, public hols 9–2 👆 Inexpensive; free to EU citizens

Museo del Baile Flamenco

Owned by the legendary flamenco dancer Cristina Hoyos, the flamenco museum includes fabulous audio-

visual and multi-media displays
explaining the history, culture and soul
of Spanish flamenco.

✉ Calle Manuel Rojas Marcos 3 ☎ 954 24
03 11 🕓 Daily 9–6 💷 Inexpensive

Museo de Bellas Artes

Housed in the former Convento de
la Merced, the museum contains a
splendid collection of fine art, including
works of art by some of the great
Spanish masters, including Zurbarán
and Murillo.

✉ Plaza de América ☎ 954 23 24 01
🕓 Wed–Sat 9–8, Tue 3–8, Sun, public hols
9–2 💷 Inexpensive; free to EU citizens

Reales Alcázares

Former Moorish palaces, largely rebuilt
for Christian kings after the reconquest
of Sevilla: the centrepiece, Palacio
Mudéjar del Rey Don Pedro, built by
Pedro I in the 14th century, is a superb
example of Mudéjar art. Salons,
archways and columns are richly
decorated with exquisite carvings,
ceramics and wooden ceilings. Note
the domed ceiling of the Salón de
Embassadores (Hall of Ambassadors).

✉ Plaza del Triunfo ☎ 954 50 23 23
🕓 Tue–Sat 9:30–7, Sun 9:30–5
💷 Moderate 🚌 C1, C2, C3, C4 ❓ Go early
if possible. Restrictions on numbers allowed
in during busy periods can result in queues

TARIFA

To stand on the Punta de Tarifa is to be at the southernmost point of Europe, with the coast of the African continent only 14km (9 miles) away. Situated on the fringe of the Costa del Sol, Tarifa has a totally different atmosphere about it which in itself makes a visit worthwhile.

The town has played an important role in the history of the Iberian Peninsula. It was named after Tarif Ibn Malik, the Moorish leader who in AD710 arrived here from North Africa with a small band of men and took possession of the area. This led to the larger invasion which took place the following year and the subsequent Moorish conquest of most of present-day Spain. Tarifa was taken by the Christians in 1292 but the siege was maintained for the next couple of years.

Entrance to the town, which is encircled by walls, is through a Moorish gate. With its dazzling white houses and maze of narrow, winding streets, Tarifa retains a distinctive Moorish look. The port offers a good view of the old Moorish castle above the town, which is in the hands of the Spanish Navy and not open to the public.

Tarifa has a long expanse of sandy beach backed by pine trees. This marks the meeting point of the Mediterranean and the Atlantic and the strong winds that sweep across the sand create excellent conditions for windsurfing in the bay. The place has now become a top centre for the sport, with kitesurfing also fast gaining in popularity.

www.tarifaweb.com

✚ 15M ✉ 21km (13 miles) west of Algeciras ⑪ Choice of restaurants (€–€€€) 🚍 Bus connections with Algeciras 🎉 Día de los Reyes (6 Jan); Carnival (pre-Lent); Romería del Consejo (15 May); Fiesta de San Juan (24 Jun); Fiesta de la Virgen del Carmen (16 Jul); National Folk Music Festival (early Aug); Fiesta de Nuestra Señora de la Luz (early Sep)

ℹ Paseo de la Alameda ☎ 956 68 09 93

a drive to Antequera

This drive offers striking scenery, taking you first to Antequera and continuing to the bizarre rock formations in the El Torcal National Park.

From Torremolinos turn onto the N340 towards Málaga. Passing the airport on your left, continue on the Málaga ring road (Ronda de Málaga) and follow the signs to Antequera (N331).

After the turn off to Finca de la Concepción, this excellent highway climbs up through the hills of the Montes de Málaga, scattered with olive groves and tiny white houses. As you approach Antequera dramatic rock shapes rise from

the fertile plains, noticeably the striking form of the so-called Peña de los Enamorados (Lovers' Rock). About an hour after departure you should enter Antequera (➤ 104–105). Allow time to explore this attractive city of churches and convents.

Take the Calle de la Legión in a southerly direction and a few moments out of town pause to admire the magnificent views of Antequera on your left, backed by the distinctive form of the Peña de los Enamorados. Take the C3310, following the signs to Torcal.

The road winds through a barren landscape of rocks and boulders for about half an hour before reaching a right turn to Parque Natural Torcal de Antequera. As you drive through the park, the shapes become increasingly curious, until the whole landscape appears positively lunar-like. The road ends about 15 minutes later by the information centre; walking trails start from here.

Rejoin the C3310 and continue south to the coast and return to Torremolinos.

Distance 125km (77.5 miles)
Time About 6 hours
Start/end point Torremolinos ✚ 20L
Lunch Parador de Antequera (€€) ✉ García del Olmo, Antequera
☎ 952 84 02 61

TORREMOLINOS

Torremolinos, lying only 8km (5 miles) west of Málaga airport, heralds the start of the most developed part of the coast. To many, this stretch of coast, lined with high-rise apartment blocks and development as far as Estepona, represents the real Costa del Sol.

Torremolinos began to grow as a holiday resort in the 1950s, when the building of luxury hotels got under way, and it became one of the first places on this coast to cater for mass tourism. Its proximity to Málaga airport is a point in its favour. At the height of summer the resort has a great appeal for the younger set, with a reputation for its hectic nightlife. Out of season, however, it takes on a different mantle. The pace slows down and, at weekends in particular, the city appears almost like a suburb, with Spanish families much in evidence.

There's a definite divide between the town and the beach area below. The main artery of the town is the pedestrian-only Calle San Miguel. Lined with a varied assortment of shops and surrounded by numerous bars and restaurants, this mini *ramblas* attracts a constant flow of people. Other popular spots for eating and drinking are the small Andalucian-style development of Pueblo Blanco nearby, and the area of El Calvario, beyond the top end of San Miguel. A favourite establishment here is the Galloping Major (splendidly translated as El Comandante Galopando), which opened in 1964 as the first English-style pub in Torremolinos.

At the south end of San Miguel the Cuesta del Tajo leads down winding steps filled with souvenir shops to the El Bajondillo beach.

The beach area shows another side of Torremolinos. With massive hotels, apartment blocks, bars and restaurants, this area is packed during the summer. To the left, the Playa de Bajondillo gives way to the beaches of Playamar and Los Alamos. To the right, beyond the Castillo de Santa Clara, lie the beach areas of La Carihuela and Montemar.

The Paseo Marítimo, the seafront promenade, extends east to Playamar and west to La Carihuela, continuing as far as

Benalmádena Costa. The walk to La Carihuela offers pleasant sea views and some dramatic rock formations, before entering the old fishing village of La Carihuela, which is a delightful area of picturesque little houses and streets. It has a good reputation for excellent fish and seafood restaurants. In summer, the *chiringuitos* (beach bars) are well worth sampling.

A pioneer of the development of Torremolinos was an Englishman. George Langworthy (Don Jorge or El Señor Inglés as he was called by the local people) made history when in 1930 he opened up his home, the Hacienda Santa Clara, as a residence for foreigners, creating a centre for the needy. He grew to be held in great esteem by the

local people and, after his death, a street was named for him and a monument erected in his honour.

www.ayto-torremolinos.org

🚻 20L 📧 12km (7.5 miles) west of Málaga 🍴 Many pubs, restaurants, bars (€–€€€) 🚆 Half-hourly to Málaga (25 minutes) and Fuengirola ❓ Carnival (pre-Lent); Feria de Verdiales (Mar); Easter; Fiesta de la Virgen del Carmen (16 Jul); Día del Turista (early Sep); Feria de San Miguel (late Sep); Romería de San Miguel (Sun, late Sep)

ℹ️ Main office: Plaza Blas Infante 1 ☎ 952 37 95 12; Plaza de la Independencia, s/n ☎ 952 37 42 31; Playa de Bajondillo ☎ 952 37 19 09

HOTELS

ANTEQUERA
Coso San Francisco (€)
Housed in a 17th-century building, the rooms have dark wood furnishings and are set around a central terrace with a restaurant.
⊠ Calle Calzada ☎ 952 84 00 14; www.cososanfrancisco.com

BENALMÁDENA COSTA
Bali Hotel (€)
Popular family hotel close to restaurants, nightlife and the port.
⊠ Avenida De Telefonica 7 ☎ 952 44 19 40

Triton (€€)
Long-established hotel set in subtropical gardens, with mountain and sea views. Pools and tennis courts.
⊠ Avenida Antonio Machado 29 ☎ 952 44 32 40

CÓRDOBA
Amistad Córdoba (€€€)
Two 18th-century mansions have been stylishly converted with Mudéjar courtyard, carved-wood ceiling and spacious rooms.
⊠ Plaza de Maimónides 3 ☎ 957 29 80 66; www.nh-hoteles.com

Mezquita (€€)
Housed in a 16th-century house opposite the mosque.
⊠ Plaza Santa Cataline 1 ☎ 957 47 55 85

ESTEPONA
Albero Lodge (€€)
Boutique hotel with each room named after a city with decor to match. Private terraces and direct access to beach.
⊠ Urbanización Finca La Cancelada, Calle Tamesis 16 ☎ 952 88 07 00; www.alberolodge.com

Atalaya Park (€€€)
Set in gardens facing the beach, with extensive sports facilities.
⊠ Carretera N340 ☎ 952 88 90 00; www.atalaya-park.es

Las Dunas Beach Hotel & Spa (€€€)

On the beach, between Marbella and Estepona. Tropical gardens, Andalucian-style decor with Middle Eastern influence. Pool, gourmet restaurant, water sports, riding, beauty and therapy clinic.

✉ La Boladilla Baja, Carretera de Cádiz, Km163.5 ☎ 952 79 43 45; www.las-dunas.com

Hostal El Pilar (€)

This small, family-run hotel, on the old town's prettiest square, has plain, comfortable rooms in a characterful old house.

✉ Plaza de las Flores 10 ☎ 952 80 00 18

El Paraíso (€€€)

Set on a hill with good views of the coast and attractive gardens, surrounded by a golf course. Outdoor and heated pool, riding.

✉ Carretera de Cádiz, Km134 ☎ 952 88 30 00; www.hotelparaisoestepona.com

FUENGIROLA

Hostal Italia (€)

Situated in the centre of town, right off the main plaza and near the beach, this small hotel is popular with its bright rooms and roof terrace.

✉ Calle de la Cruz 1 ☎ 952 47 41 93

Villa de Laredo (€€)

At the quieter end of the promenade, across from the beach, Villa de Laredo has an old-fashioned feel but is excellent value given its location and facilities.

✉ Paseo Marítimo 42 ☎ 952 47 76 89; www.hotelvilladelaredo.com

GIBRALTAR

Bristol (€€)

A colonial-style hotel with views of the bay and the cathedral. Rooms are spacious and comfortable and the adjacent garden is a tropical haven.

✉ 10 Cathedral Square ☎ 200 76 800; www.bristolhotel.gi

The Rock (€€€)
Dating back to 1932, this colonial-style hotel has excellent rooms and a fine terrace bar with a wisteria-covered terrace.
✉ 3 Europa Road ☎ 200 73 000; www.rockhotelgibraltar.com

MARBELLA
Andalucía Plaza (€€)
Spacious establishment, attractively refurbished. Set in gardens with two pools and a casino.
✉ Nueva Andalucía (opposite Puerto Banús) ☎ 952 81 20 00

Artola (€€)
Pretty hotel with yellow trim and green shutters. Rooms have balconies and there is a 9-hole golf course, pool and nearby beach.
✉ Carretera de Cádiz, Km194 ☎ 952 93 13 90; www.hotelartola.com

Hotel Fuerte Miramar-Spa (€€€)
Part of the El Fuerte group, this modern hotel on the seafront has an outdoor heated pool, hydrotherapy centre and good facilities.
✉ Plaza José Luque Manzano, s/n ☎ 952 76 84 10; www.fuertehoteles.com

Marbella Club (€€€)
Luxurious old-time favourite, set in lush gardens with swimming pool, restaurants, beach bar and boutiques.
✉ Boulevard Príncipe Alfonso de Hohenlohe ☎ 952 82 22 11;
www.marbellaclub.com

Puente Romano (€€€)
This palatial hotel is designed like an Andalucian *pueblo*, complete with gardens and fountains. Four restaurants plus a beach club.
✉ Carretera N340, between Marbella and Puerto Banús ☎ 952 82 09 00;
www.puenteromano.com

Riu Rincón Andaluz (€€)
Attractive hotel complex built in an Andalucian-style *pueblo*. Near Puerto Banús and close to the sea.
✉ Carretera de Cádiz, Km173 ☎ 952 81 15 17; www.riu.com

MIJAS
TRH Mijas (€€)
At the entrance to Mijas, the hotel is set amid gardens with a poolside restaurant and bar, offering superb views down to the coast.

✉ Urbanizacíon Tamisa, s/n ☎ 952 48 58 0

MONDA
Castillo de Monda (€€)
Castle converted into a hotel by British proprietors. Moorish-style furnishings, stunning views of Monda and the Sierra de las Nieves.

✉ Monda (18km/11 miles northeast of Marbella) ☎ 952 45 71 42; www.mondacastle.com

RONDA
Ancinipo (€€)
The artistic legacy of former owners and local artists is in evidence throughout this boutique hotel, which has many murals and paintings. The creative, modern interior has exposed stone panels, steel-and-glass fittings, and mosaic-tile bathrooms.

✉ José Aparico 7 ☎ 952 16 10 02; www.hotelacinipo.com

Don Miguel (€€)
On the edge of the Tajo, next to the bridge. Some rooms have spectacular views of the gorge.

✉ Villanueva 4 ☎ 952 87 77 22; www.dmiguel.com

San Gabriel (€€)
Delightful hotel stylishly furnished with antiques, housed in an 18th-century mansion with an attractive courtyard.

✉ Marqués de Moctezuma 19 ☎ 952 19 03 92; www.hotelsangabriel.com

SAN PEDRO DE ALCÁNTARA
Breakers Lodge (€€)
A small British-owned hotel near the beach with pool, terraces and comfortable, good-sized rooms. Located in a quiet residential area.

✉ Avenida Las Mimosas 189, Linda Vista Baja ☎ 952 78 47 80

SEVILLA

Alfonso XIII (€€€)
One of Spain's most famous hotels. Built around a large courtyard with arches and greenery. Moorish-style with marble floors, panelled ceilings and lovely ceramic tiles. Gardens and pool.
✉ Calle San Fernando 2 ☎ 954 91 70 00; www.westin.com/hotelalfonso

Hostería del Laurel (€€)
In the heart of the picturesque Barrio de Santa Cruz. Has an outdoor restaurant in a square lined with pretty houses.
✉ Plaza de los Venerables 5 ☎ 954 22 02 95; www.hosteriadellaurel.com

Hotel Alminar (€)
Although this hotel is new, it manages to present a wonderfully traditional atmosphere. Rooms are spacious and well-equipped.
✉ Álvarez Quintero 52 ☎ 954 29 39 13; www.hotelalminar.com

TORREMOLINOS

Cabello (€)
This small, whitewashed hotel is a block from the beach. The rooms have few frills, but most have impressive sea views.
✉ Chiriva 28, La Carihuela ☎ 952 28 45 05

Hotel El Pozo (€€)
Traditional whitewashed hotel, close to the beach. Facilities include private balconies, satellite TV, a library and bar/cafeteria.
✉ Calle Casablanca 2 ☎ 952 38 06 22; www.hotelpozo.com

Miami (€)
Small 1950 hotel, designed by Manolo Blascos, Picasso's cousin. Surrounded by a shady garden; a stay is like visiting a local home.
✉ Aladino 14 ☎ 952 38 52 55; www.residencia-miami.com

Pez Espada (€€)
This large hotel offers all comforts, with a pool and gardens.
✉ Avenida Salvador Allende 11, La Carihuela ☎ 952 38 03 00; www.hotelpezespadamalaga.com

RESTAURANTS

ANTEQUERA

El Angelote (€€)

Atmospheric restaurant with two wood-beamed dining rooms.
Try the wild mushrooms in an almond and wine sauce.

✉ Plaza Coso Viejo ☎ 952 70 34 65 🕐 Lunch and dinner

Coso San Francisco (€)

Part of the hotel of the same name, this restaurant has a minstrel-
style gallery, original tiles and open fireplace. The menu includes
beef and pork dishes, plus spicy cod *pil pil* and vegetarian options.

✉ Calle Calzada 27 ☎ 952 84 00 14 🕐 Lunch and dinner

ARROYO DE LA MIEL

Ventorillo de la Perra (€€€)

Housed in an 18th-century inn. Cosy, attractive patio with plants.
Spanish and international dishes.

✉ Avenida de la Constitución 85 ☎ 952 44 19 66 🕐 Lunch and dinner;
closed Mon

BENALMÁDENA COSTA

Airen (€€€)

This elegant restaurant is owned by the same people as the
Michelin-starred Café de Paris in Málaga, and the dishes are
as innovative and stylish.

✉ Reserva del Higuerón ☎ 952 56 58 84 🕐 Dinner only; closed Sun

Mar de Alborán (€€)

Sophisticated restaurant serving Basque-inspired seafood dishes,
including hake stew with clams.

✉ Avenida de Alay 5 ☎ 952 44 64 27 🕐 Lunch and dinner

BENALMÁDENA PUEBLO

Casa Fidel (€€)

Popular restaurant in a typical Andalucian house with arches, patio
and terracotta tiles. The menu is contemporary Mediterranean.

✉ Maestra Ayala 1 ☎ 952 44 91 65 🕐 Lunch and dinner; closed Tue

CÓRDOBA
Bandelero (€–€€)
Facing the Mezquita with an attractively decorated bar and several dining rooms at the rear. Wide range of simple dishes and *tapas*.

✉ Calle de Torrijos 6 ☎ 957 47 64 91 🕔 Lunch and dinner

Bodega Campos (€€)
A refreshingly untouristy restaurant with a superb atmosphere. The rustic-style dining room is lined with barrels and the menu includes grilled meats and *salmorejo*.

✉ Calle Lineros ☎ 952 49 75 00 🕔 Lunch and dinner; closed Sun eve

ESTEPONA
Buenaventura (€€€)
Top-quality restaurant offering creative cuisine. Dine in the courtyard and on the plaza (operatic performances in August).

✉ Plaza de la Iglesia 5 ☎ 952 85 80 69 🕔 Lunch and dinner

El Cenachero (€€)
Mediterranean cuisine, specializes in fresh shellfish, *zarzuelas* and fish baked in salt.

✉ Puerto Deportivo ☎ 952 80 14 42 🕔 Lunch and dinner; closed Tue in winter and 15–30 Nov

El Gavilan del Mar (€€)
Located right on an attractive square, this seafood restaurant has appropriately nautical decor and a menu including lobster bisque and paella.

✉ Calle Correo Viejo 1 ☎ 952 80 28 56 🕔 Lunch and dinner; closed Sun

FUENGIROLA
Bar Tipi Tapa (€)
You can happily (and cheaply) fill up with tasty tapas here – it's what they do best. Choose from a selection including anchovies in vinaigrette, fried potatoes in garlic mayonnaise, stuffed eggs with tuna and much more. Located right off the main shopping street.

✉ Calle Pintor Nogales ☎ 952 19 92 36 🕔 Lunch and dinner

Café Fresco (€)

An excellent lunchtime choice with its healthy salad bar, home-made soups, baguettes, sandwiches and wraps; the latter include Thai chicken salad, Greek salad and chicken Caesar.

✉ Las Rampas ☎ 635 86 37 91 🕔 Mon–Sat 9–4

La Langosta (€€)

Long-established favourite with a stylish art deco interior; renowned for its lobster dishes.

✉ Calle Francisco Cano 1, Los Boliches ☎ 952 47 50 49 🕔 Dinner only; closed Sun

GIBRALTAR
The Clipper (€)

An authentic pubby atmosphere with tasty grub like fish and chips, steak and ale pie, and home-made soup with crusty bread.

✉ 78b Irish Town ☎ 200 79 791 🕔 Lunch and dinner

Gauchos (€€)

The diverse menu here includes Argentinian grills, baked blue cheese in pastry and salmon with grilled banana, mango and avocado.

✉ Waterport Casemates ☎ 200 59 700 🕔 Lunch and dinner

MARBELLA
El Bálcon de la Virgen

See page 58.

California (€)

Casual ambience, popular with locals. Good-value fish and seafood *tapas*.

✉ Calle Málaga 2, Edificio Sol No 2 ☎ 952 86 67 52 🕔 Lunch and dinner, closed Sun

La Hacienda (€€€)

Top restaurant with reputation for *haute cuisine*. Enjoys a good hilltop location with sea views.

✉ Urbanización Las Chapas, N340 (12km/7.5 miles east of Marbella) ☎ 952 83 11 16 🕐 Dinner only in summer; closed Mon, Tue and mid-Nov to mid-Dec

La Pesquera del Faro (€€)

Overlooking the sea, this combines the atmosphere of a beach hotel with good-quality food. Specials include fish baked in salt and seafood dishes. Steps lead down to a terrace right on the beach, adjoining Marbella's marina.

✉ Playa del Faro, Paseo del Marítimo ☎ 952 86 85 20 🕐 Lunch and dinner

Santiago (€€)

See page 59.

Zozoi (€€)

Creative cuisine with fusion starters such as Thai fishcakes with fresh rocket (arugula) salad, plus more than 45 different vodkas, as well as some unusual wines and liqueurs.

✉ Plaza Altamirano 1 ☎ 952 76 90 30 🕐 Lunch and dinner

MIJAS

Bar Porras (€)

At the base of the most photographed street in the village, this attracts a regular crowd of locals with its good-value, tasty *tapas*. Outside seating in summer.

✉ Plaza de la Libertad ☎ No phone 🕐 Lunch and dinner

Mirlo Blanco (€€)

Basque and international cuisine. The outdoor terrace overlooks the little square of Plaza de la Constitución.

✉ Plaza de la Constitución 2 ☎ 952 48 57 00 🕐 Lunch and dinner; closed Jan

El Padrastro (€€€)

Spectacularly sited on the clifftop. Terrace with views of Fuengirola and the coast. Top cuisine, offers local specialities and international dishes. Access by lift or a steep flight of stairs.

✉ Paseo del Compás 22 ☎ 952 48 50 00 🕐 Lunch and dinner

Valparaíso (€€)

In an attractive villa with a terrace, gardens and a pool, this is ideal for a dinner-dancing evening out.

✉ Carretera de Fuengirola, Km 4 ☎ 952 48 59 96 🕓 Dinner only; closed Sun in winter

NUEVA ANDALUCÍA

Magna Café (€€)

Attracts a loyal following for the inspirational cuisine of young Latvian chef Edmund Cicans. The international menu includes Italian dishes such as tuna and salmon carpaccio.

✉ Magna Marbella Golf, Nueva Andalucía ☎ 952 92 95 78 🕓 Lunch and dinner

PUERTO BANÚS

Azul Marino (€€€)

Brasserie-restaurant with a large terrace, good for fish and seafood.

✉ Front Line, Port 1 ☎ 952 21 70 78 🕓 Lunch and dinner

Dalli's (€€)

One of several Dalli family restaurants, this is run by son, Simon, and has an extensive menu of authentic and innovative pasta and pizza dishes and a fashionable dining space.

✉ Second Line, Port 1 ☎ 952 21 70 78 🕓 Lunch and dinner

Don Leone (€€€)

Longtime open-air favourite overlooking the marina and serving creative Italian cuisine.

✉ Muelle Ribera ☎ 952 81 17 16 🕓 Lunch and dinner; closed end Nov–end Dec

Egan's Bar Restaurant (€€)

Home-cooked fresh food with a creative flair. Dishes include sardine and plum tomato *bruscheta* and vegetable *tagine* served with cinnamon cous cous.

✉ Avenida Los Girasoles ☎ 952 81 46 73 🕓 Lunch and dinner

SAN PEDRO DE ALCÁNTARA

The Birdcage (€€)

This venue provides an evening's drag show entertainment, along with its set four-course menu. The menu changes weekly, but typical dishes include prawn and swordfish with lemon risotto and grilled salmon.

✉ Los Almendros ☎ 952 92 77 22 🕐 Lunch and dinner; closed Sun–Wed

Gambasol (€€)

Family-run restaurant specializing in Scandinavian and English dishes, including Swedish meatballs, gravlax with creamed dill potatoes and soya-glazed spare ribs.

✉ Urbanización Las Petunias ☎ 952 78 82 12 🕐 Lunch and dinner; closed Wed

Passion Café (€)

Serves international food in a relaxed atmosphere. Menu includes burritos, fajitas, stir fries, chicken with satay sauce, Thai prawns.

✉ Comercial La Colonia ☎ 952 78 15 83 🕐 Daily

Victor (€€)

Specialities include rack of lamb, sea bass and good seafood.

✉ Centro Comercial Guadalmina, local 1 ☎ 952 88 34 91 🕐 Lunch and dinner; closed Sun dinner and Mon

SAN ROQUE

Los Remos (€€€)

High-class restaurant in a neoclassical villa with attractive gardens. Known for fish and seafood dishes.

✉ Villa Victoria S, Campamento ☎ 956 69 84 12 🕐 Lunch and dinner; closed Sun

SEVILLA

La Albahaca (€€)

Housed in a stately Andalucian manor house, decorated with tiles, antiques and plants. Spanish and French cuisine.

✉ Plaza Santa Cruz 12 ☎ 954 22 07 14 🕐 Lunch and dinner; closed Sun

Casa Robles (€€)

Traditional restaurant near the cathedral. Classic Andalucian dishes and lively *tapas* bar downstairs, frequented by locals.

✉ Calle Álvarez Quinters 58 ☎ 954 56 32 72 🕐 Lunch and dinner

El Giraldillo (€€)

Well-established restaurant facing the cathedral and Giralda. Tables on the pavement for a drink and a light meal.

✉ Plaza Virgen de los Reyes 2 ☎ 954 21 45 25 🕐 Lunch and dinner

Taberna del Alabardero (€€)

Delightful restaurant in a 19th-century villa serving modern dishes such as grilled cod with mushrooms in a spicy chilli and ham sauce. Fronted by a bar and terrace for alfresco dining.

✉ Zaragoza 20 ☎ 954 56 06 37 🕐 Lunch and dinner

TORREMOLINOS

Bodegas Quitapeñas (€€)

Reliably excellent traditional *bodega* serving seafood *tapas* and ice-cold *fino* straight from the barrel.

✉ Cuesta del Tajo 4 ☎ 952 38 62 44 🕐 Lunch and dinner

La Chacha (€)

This open-air seafood *tapas* bar is an institution. Stand to sample its wide range of fresh fish and seafood.

✉ Palma de Mallorca 3 ☎ None 🕐 Lunch and dinner

Golden Curry (€)

One of the best Indian restaurants on the Costa del Sol. All the familiar dishes are here, and a terrace overlooks the streets below.

✉ La Nogalera Bloque 6 ☎ 952 37 48 55 🕐 Lunch and dinner

La Jábega (€€)

This lively restaurant along the promenade serves a good choice of meat, fish and seafood.

✉ Paseo Marítimo, La Carihuela ☎ 952 38 63 75 🕐 Lunch and dinner

Med (€€)

Central restaurant with a cool sophisticated ambience and the emphasis on Mediterranean cuisine. Panoramic views.

✉ La Mercedes 12, 2a Planta ☎ 952 05 88 30 ⏰ Lunch and dinner; closed Mon

La Zoca (€€)

La Zoca overlooks a pretty stretch of beach and specialities include the local *malagueño* dish *freiduria* – light and crispy tempura-style seafood.

✉ Bulto 61, Paseo Marítimo, La Carihuela ☎ 952 38 59 25 ⏰ Lunch and dinner; closed Tue

SHOPPING

BENALMÁDENA (PUERTO MARINA)

Andycraft

Great for gift ideas, including imported masks, statues and decorative items from Indonesia, plus locally produced crafts.

✉ Paseo Marítimo, local 1 ☎ 952 57 40 66

ESTEPONA

Babilonia Collection

Lots of unusual gifts, including exquisite Japanese tea sets, frames, hammocks, jewellery, sculpture and artwork.

✉ Calle Real, Edificio Nadal 6 ☎ 952 79 80 07

Cerámica La Chiminea

Beautiful designs created by Paco Leonicio, who learned his crafts at Triana, one of Spain's top centres for pottery. Wide selection of hand-painted tiles, glazed and unglazed ceramics.

✉ Calle El Cerrillo 6 ☎ 952 79 44 75

FUENGIROLA

Bookworld España

English-language bookshop with the latest bestsellers, plus guidebooks to Spain and Andalucía and coffee-table books.

✉ Avenida Jesus Santos Rein, s/n ☎ 952 66 48 37

Bravo

Good reputation for shoes, handbags, luggage and leather accessories. Shops also in Marbella and Torremolinos.
✉ Avenida Condes de San Isidro 33 ☎ 952 46 17 19

Nicholson

Specializes in modern jewellery designs, mainly in silver.
✉ Calle Marbella, s/n ☎ 952 47 58 82

GIBRALTAR

Gibraltar Arts and Crafts

Quality handmade souvenirs and gift items, including glass paintings, jewellery, woodwork, sculpture, jams and chutneys.
✉ 15b Casemates Square ☎ 200 73 865

Red Skins

Specialists in leather, with coats, bags and hats for sale.
✉ 97 Main Street ☎ 200 71 667

MARBELLA

Antonio Seijo

One of the longest-established fine jewellery shops on the coast.
✉ Avenida Ramón y Cajal 7 ☎ 952 90 01 40

La Cañada Commercial Centre

Individual shops, fast-food restaurants and a supermarket.
✉ Parque Comerical la Cañada, Carretera de Ojén, s/n ☎ 952 86 01 42

Charles Jourdan

Wide range of shoes and leather goods. Other items include jewellery, umbrellas and sun glasses.
✉ Avenida Ramón y Cajal ☎ 952 77 00 03

Don Miguel

Long established, with wide range of fashionwear for men and women. Some of the brand names to be found here.
✉ Avenida Ricardo Soriano 5 ☎ 952 77 31 40

Grutman
Carpets, rugs, runners and kilims. Worldwide shipment available.
✉ Carretera de Cádiz, Km179 ☎ 952 82 72 20; www.grutman.com

Louis Feraud
Fashion clothes by Feraud, known for striking designs and vibrant colours.
✉ Plaza Victoria ☎ 952 82 81 06

Semon
Quality deli selling a wide range of items, including national and imported cheeses, caviar, smoked salmon and cold meats. Small bar for salads, healthy sandwiches and drinks.
✉ Gregorio Marañon, s/n ☎ 952 57 61 72

PUERTO BANÚS
Aftershock
A boutique that specializes in flouncy, sequined eveningwear for women, imported from London, India, Italy and France.
✉ Plaza Marina Banús ☎ 952 81 27 62

Costa Marbella Department Stores
Gigantic superstore, just outside town. Part of the El Corte Inglés chain, with a hypermarket and specialized shops.
✉ Carretera N340, Km174 ☎ 952 90 99

RONDA
Muñoz Soto
Sells a range of antiques.
✉ B S Juan de Dios de Córdoba 34 ☎ 952 87 14 51

SAN PEDRO DE ALCÁNTARA
Anthony's Jewellers
Unusual and original designs by the owner.
✉ Plaza las Faroles ☎ 952 78 62 74

Casa
Stylish houseware and gift ideas for the home.
✉ Avenida del Rocio, s/n ☎ 952 78 91 98

Rialsa Antiques
Fine antiques, at the higher end of the market, plus original artwork.
✉ San Antonio entre Manuel Cantos y Badajoz ☎ 677 62 21 89

SEVILLA
Sevillarte
A wide range of ceramic products at three different branches.
✉ Branches at: Gloria 5 ☎ 954 21 88 35; Sierpes 66 ☎ 954 21 28 36; Vida 13 ☎ 954 56 29 45

TORREMOLINOS
Geny
These Lladro porcelain figurines make excellent gifts. This shop has a large showroom with pieces ranging from graceful dancers to the spiritual icons collection.
✉ Calle San Miguel 8 ☎ 952 38 28 05

Misako
The fashionable bags here are excellent value and, although most are synthetic, they look and feel like real leather.
✉ Calle San Miguel 2 ☎ 952 05 62 36

Los Quatros Hermanos
Specializes in leather handbags, coats and clothing.
✉ Paseo Marítimo 45, La Carihuela ☎ 952 05 50 664

Las Tres Torres
Offers a good choice of products, including items made in Toledo steel, ceramics and pottery from Sevilla, and an attractive selection of Mallorcan pearls.
✉ Calle San Miguel 17 ☎ 952 21 79 39

ENTERTAINMENT

BENALMÁDENA COSTA

Casino Torrequebrada

American and French roulette, Black Jack, Punto Blanco, slot machines and private gaming room. Dress is formal and passports must be shown.

✉ Avenida del Sol, s/n ☎ 952 44 60 00 🕐 Daily 8pm–4am 🚌 Bus stop Benalmádena Costa 💷 Expensive

Fortuna Nightclub

See page 78.

CÓRDOBA

Tablao Cardenal

See page 78.

FUENGIROLA

Cine Sur Fuengirola Miramar

Original-version films shown daily.

✉ Avenida de la Encarnación, Parque Miramar ☎ 952 19 86 00

Discoteca Maxy

A late-night disco for a more mature crowd.

✉ Calle España ☎ No phone

Moochers Jazz Club

Very popular café and restaurant. Live music every evening in summer, from jazz to rock. Terrace.

✉ Calle de la Cruz 17 ☎ 952 47 71 54 🕐 Dinner only

Salon Variétés

Cinema and theatre with regular plays and entertainment for the English-speaking community.

✉ Emancipación 30 ☎ 952 47 45 42

GIBRALTAR
Lord Nelson
The Rock's favourite venue for live music, including jam sessions from Wednesday to Sunday, plus Wednesday karaoke.

✉ 10 Casemates Square ☎ 200 44 307

The Tunnel
A bar/restaurant by day, the Tunnel's nocturnal flipside is a popular music bar with a healthy mix of music ranging from classic rock to hip hop and jazz.

✉ 8 Casemates Square ☎ 200 74 946

MARBELLA
Ana Maria
See pages 78–79.

La Caseta del Casino
Shows of flamenco dancing and *sevillanas*.

✉ Casino Nueva Andalucía, Andalucía Plaza Hotel, N340, Nueva Andalucía.
☎ 952 81 40 00 ◉ From midnight in summer

Casino Marbella
American and French roulette, Black Jack, Stud Caribbean poker, Punto Blanco, slot machines. Jacket and tie for men. Passport required.

✉ Hotel Andalucía Plaza, opposite Puerto Banús, Nueva Andalucía ☎ 952 81 40 00 ◉ Daily 9pm–3am 🚌 Bus stop Andalucía Plaza ✋ Expensive

Cine Sur Plaza del Marbella
Original-version films shown daily.

✉ Avenida Camilo José Cela ☎ 952 76 69 42

La Notte
Seriously glam late-night club for big spenders who like it loud.

✉ Casals 17 ☎ 952 86 69 96

Olivia Valere
Looks like a Moorish palace (inside and out) and is, without doubt, the place on the Costa to be seen strutting your stuff.
✉ Carretera de Istán, Km0.8 ☎ 952 82 88 45

NEUVA ANDALUCÍA
Casino Nueva San Roque
Chic casino. Passport, jacket and tie required.
✉ Carretera N340, Km127 ☎ 965 78 10 00

PUERTO BANÚS
Cine Gran Marbella
You can see films in English at this multiplex.
✉ Puerto Banús ☎ 952 81 00 77

Dreamers
Popular venue playing a good variety of music.
✉ A7, Km175 ☎ 952 81 20 80

Navy Disco Bar
Improve your dance moves in a non-stop party atmosphere at one of the longest-running clubs in the port, with regular live bands.
✉ 2nd Line ☎ 952 81 71 70

RONDA
Circulo de Artistas
See page 79.

SEVILLA
El Arenal
See page 79.

Los Gallos
See page 79.

Teatro Lope de Vega
For classical concerts.
✉ Avenida María Luisa, s/n ☎ 954 59 08 53

Teatro Municipal Alameda
Varied programme of plays.
✉ Calle Crédito 13 ☎ 954 38 83 12

TORREMOLINOS
Fun Beach
This claims to be the largest disco in Europe with eight dance floors.
✉ Avenida Palma de Mallorca ☎ 952 38 02 56

Palladium
A popular spot, with trendy lighting and loud music.
✉ Avenida Palma de Mallorca 36 ☎ 952 38 42 89

Taberna Flamenco Pepe López
See page 79.

SPORT

BENALMÁDENA COSTA
Club Nautico Diving Centre
Year-round diving courses, equipment hire included. Daily trips from the marina.
✉ Puerto Marina de Benalmádena ☎ 952 56 07 69

Club de Tenis Torrequebrada
✉ Urbanizacíon Torrequebrada, Carretera de Cádiz Km220 ☎ 952 44 27 42

Torrequebrada Golf
Par 72 18-hole course, plus a 9-hole course.
✉ Carretera de Cádiz, N340, Km 220 ☎ 952 44 27 42;
www.golftorrequebrada.com

ESTEPONA
Atalaya Golf and Country Club
Eighteen holes, par 71 and 72.

✉ Carretera Benahavis, Km0.7 ☎ 952 88 28 12; www.atalaya-golf.com

Club de Tenis Estepona
Ten courts, three floodlit; hard and quick surfaces.

✉ Urbanizacíon Forest Hill ☎ 952 80 15 79; www.clubdetenisestepona.com

Estepona Golf
Eighteen holes, par 72.

✉ Carretera de Cádiz, N340, Km150 ☎ 952 11 30 81;
www.esteponagolf.com

Finca Siesta
Picnic and beach rides. Lessons in dressage and showjumping.

✉ Km163 on N230 (opposite Hacienda Beach) ☎ 952 79 01 89;
www.finca-siesta.com

FUENGIROLA
Aztec Tennis Club Riviera del Sol
Tennis lessons available.

✉ Urbanizacíon Riviera del Sol, Libra, s/n ☎ 952 93 44 77

Fuengirola Diving Centre
Complete PADI scuba diving courses available.

✉ Fuengirola port ☎ 952 58 83 12

Sierra Cycling
✉ Urbanizacíon Puelo Castillo 7 ☎ 952 47 17 20; www.sierracycling.com

GIBRALTAR
Dolphin Safari
A boat trip to view the dolphins with a 98 per cent guarantee that
they will be spotted. Maximum of 12 passengers.

✉ Marina Bay ☎ 609 29 04 00

MARBELLA

Cabopino Golf
Modern design with fine views of the coast. 18 holes, par 70.
✉ Urbanizacíon Artola Atta, s/n, Km194 ☎ 952 85 02 82

Centro de Tenis Don Carlos
Eleven courts, four floodlit; clay and quick surfaces.
✉ Urbanizacíon Elviria, Carretera de Cádiz ☎ 952 83 17 39

Club El Casco
Eight clay courts, including two coin-operated floodlit courts.
✉ Urbanizacíon El Rosario ☎ 952 83 76 51; www.elcaso.com

Club Hípico Elviria
✉ El Platero, between Marbella and Fuengirola ☎ 952 83 52 72

Club Hotel Los Monteros
Ten courts, two floodlit.
✉ Carretera de Cádiz, Km194 ☎ 952 77 17 00

Club Puente Romano
Five clay courts, four quick-surface and two artificial grass courts.
Several courts are also floodlit.
✉ Hotel Puente Romano, Carretera de Cádiz ☎ 952 82 61 03

La Dame de Noche Golf
A 24-hour nine-hole course. Floodlighting enables golfers to play at night as well as by day.
✉ Camino del Angel, Río Verde ☎ 952 81 81 50

Manolo Santana Raquets Club
✉ Carretera de Istán, Km2 ☎ 952 77 85 80

Marbella Golf Club
Eighteen holes, par 72.
✉ Urbanizacíon El Rosario, Carretera de Cádiz, N340, Km 192 ☎ 952 83 05 00; www.marbellagolf.com

Los Monteros Riding School
Provides lessons and rides taking in the surrounding hills.
✉ Carretera de Cádiz, N340, Km177 ☎ 952 77 06 75

MIJAS
Lew Hoad Campo de Tenis
Eight courts, quick surface. Clinics and courses are also available.
✉ Carretera de Mijas ☎ 952 47 48 58; www.tennis-spain.com

MIJAS-COSTA
La Cala Golf
Two 18-hole courses, par 72 and 73.
✉ La Cala de Mijas ☎ 952 66 90 33; www.lacala.com

Mijas Golf International
Eighteen holes, par 71 and 72.
✉ Urbanizacíon Mijas Golf ☎ 952 47 68 43; www.mijasgolf.org

Miraflores Golf
Eighteen holes, par 70. Right up in the hills of Mijas.
✉ Urbanizacíon Riviera del Sol, Carretera de Cádiz, N340, Km199
☎ 952 93 19 60; www.miraflores-golf.com

RONDA
La Quinta Golf & Country Club
Twenty-seven holes. Fine views of the mountains and Marbella
coastline. Training programmes for beginners and more advanced
players, also special courses for groups.
✉ Carretera San Pedro–Ronda, C339, Km3 ☎ 952 76 23 90;
www.laquintagolf.com

SAN PEDRO DE ALCÁNTARA
Guadalmina Club de Golf
Two 18-hole courses and a 9 hole course.
✉ Urbanizacíon Guadalmina Alta ☎ 952 88 33 75;
www.guadalminagolf.com

Lakeview Equestrian Centre

Qualified instruction in dressage and showjumping; private or group lessons.

✉ Urbanizacíon Valle del Sol ☎ 952 78 69 34

SAN ROQUE

San Roque Golf

Eighteen holes, par 72.

✉ Urbanizacíon San Roque Club, Carretera de Cádiz, N340, Km127

☎ 956 61 30 30; www.sanroqueclub.net

The San Roque Club Equestrian Centre

For beginners and experienced riders. One-hour or full-day hacks.

✉ San Roque Club Suites Hotel, Carretera Cádiz, Km126.5 ☎ 956 61 32 32

SOTOGRANDE

Real Club de Golf Sotogrande

Eighteen- and nine-hole courses. Beautiful design by Robert Trent.

✉ Paseo del Parque ☎ 956 78 50 14; www.golfsotogrande.com

TARIFA

Centro Buceo Tarifa

A wide range of scuba diving courses, day and night.

✉ Calle Alcalde Juan Nuñez 10 ☎ 956 68 16 48

Hot Stick Kite Surfing

✉ Calle Batalla del Salado 41 ☎ 956 68 04 19

TORREMOLINOS

Autos Lara Jeep Safari

Full-day jeep tours daily to El Chorro and Ardales National Park.

✉ Via Imperial 12–14 ☎ 952 38 18 00

East of Málaga

Less developed than western Málaga, this stretch of Mediterranean shoreline has a more rocky appearance, a number of pleasant beaches and attractive resorts such as Nerja. There is an appealing freshness to Nerja's old town of narrow streets, and the limestone Cuevas de Nerja are only 4km (2.5 miles) east.

Granada

Beyond the coast you will discover the essence of Andalucía among great mountain ranges, with the Sierra Nevada at the heart and the world-famous buildings of Granada which embodies Spain's Moorish past in its architectural treasures. The variety of the landscape and the charm and individuality of the people will reward those visitors who are searching for the heart and soul of southern Spain.

ALMUÑÉCAR

Almuñécar, situated in the province of Granada, within the coastline now designated as the Costa Tropical, lies amid orchards of tropical fruits. It presents a very picturesque scene, typical of so many villages to be found in southern Spain, with a cluster of whitewashed houses rising up the hillside crowned by an old castle. Its history goes back to the time of the Phoenicians, with subsequent occupation by the Romans and the Moors. The Castillo de San Miguel stands on top of a tall rock, dividing two bays. It was built during the reign of Carlos V, over the site of a former Moorish fortress, and features a great square tower known as La Mazmorra.

The town itself is a jumble of narrow, cobblestoned streets, climbing steeply up to the summit. Do not miss a visit to the Ornithological Park located at the foot of the hill. Here you can see brilliantly coloured parrots and rare species of birds in a beautiful setting of subtropical plants and flowers. The seafront is lined with apartment blocks, bars and restaurants, with a lively scene by day and night during the season.

Also worth a visit is the small archaeological museum housed in the Cueva de los Siete Palacios, thought to have been a Roman reservoir for water. The museum has a display of objects from the area (open Tue–Sat 11–2 and 6–8).

A look-out post at nearby Punta de la Mona offers sweeping views of the harbour and the Mediterranean.

✚ 23L ✉ 84km (52 miles) east of Málaga 🍴 Variety of restaurants

🚌 Local bus services

ℹ Avenida Fenicia ☎ 958 63 11 25

CÓMPETA

Way up in the mountains of La Axarquiá, the region east of Málaga, is the small town of Cómpeta, which can be reached by taking the road leading inland from Torrox-Costa.

Cómpeta is noted for its attractive setting, perched atop a mountain ridge surrounded by vineyards. It is one of a number of easily accessible Andalucian towns and villages located in the hills which offer fine views down to the coast. The town is made up of a cluster of whitewashed houses and winding streets. On the main square stands the baroque Iglesia de la Asunción, which has an impressive bell tower.

Cómpeta has a sizeable community of foreign residents, a number of whom are involved with craft industries. A big attraction is the lively wine festival which is held each year in August in the main square.

✚ 22K ✉ 51km (31.5 miles) east of Málaga 🍴 Several restaurants (€–€€)

🚌 Local services ❓ Noche del Vino (15 Aug)

ℹ Avenida de la Constitución ☎ 952 55 36 85

CUEVAS DE NERJA

Best places to see, ➤ 44–45.

FRIGILIANA

It is well worth taking a short drive of some 6km (4 miles) up into the hills from Nerja to visit Frigiliana. This pretty little village spreads its dazzlingly whitewashed houses out over the hills in two sections. The older part is a mass of narrow, cobbled streets winding their way up the hillside with wonderful views over fertile orchards and the coast. Here and there you may come across a donkey patiently carrying its load. Streets and balconies are decked out with flowers. The village continues to attract a growing number

of visitors, with more shops and restaurants springing up all over.

One of the last battles between the Christians and the Moors was fought in the area in the 16th century, resulting in victory for the Christians. The tale of this glorious event is related by way of a series of ceramic tiles on the walls of the houses.

✚ 22L ✉ 56km (35 miles) east of Málaga 🍴 Some restaurants (€€)

🚌 Local ❓ Día de la Cruz (3 May); Fería de San Antonio (13 Jun)

ℹ Plaza del Ingenio, s/n ☎ 952 53 42 61

FUENTE VAQUEROS

Fuente Vaqueros is home to the **Casa Museo García Lorca**. The museum was the former home of the poet and playwright Federico García Lorca, who was born in Fuente Vaqueros in 1898. Lorca, who spent much time in nearby Granada, became known for the sensitivity of his poetry and the powerful drama of his plays, such as *Yerma*, *Blood Wedding* and *The House of Bernarda Alba*, which continue to be widely produced on stage throughout the world. He was assassinated near Viznar during the Spanish Civil War.

✚ 23J ✉ 17km (10.5 miles) west of Granada

Casa Museo Federico García Lorca

✉ Calle Poeta García Lorca 4 ☎ 958 51 64 53; www.museogarcialorca.org 🕐 Tue–Sun 10–1, 4–8 (winter 4–6). Tours hourly 💰 Inexpensive

GRANADA

Granada is the capital of its province, the seat of an archbishop and a university town. In addition to La Alhambra, with which Granada is so closely associated, the city has much else to commend it: its beautiful setting, built on three hills backed by the snowy peaks of the Sierra Nevada, its historic links with the past and significant religious festivals. A visit to Granada could be made from the coast within a day. However, more time is recommended to explore one of Spain's crowning glories, the last kingdom of the Moors.

Known as Iliberis during the Iberian culture, Granada was taken by the Romans and the Visigoths before its conquest by the Moors in 711. The 11th century saw the decline of the Caliphate of Córdoba and the beginning of the Kingdom of Granada. From the 13th century, until its downfall at the end of the 15th century, Granada flourished as a prosperous cultural centre with the construction of magnificent buildings such as La Alhambra (► 38–39). In 1492 Granada was taken by the Catholic Monarchs. This marked the end of Moorish rule and Spain's history was changed. Granada continued to prosper during the Renaissance but declined after the repression of a Moorish uprising in the 16th century.

The priority for most visitors is the palace of La Alhambra. Magical as this Moorish palace is, it is surrounded by some equally fascinating places. The summer palace of El Generalife, with its shady avenues, water gardens, fountains and airy gazebos, is a neighbour of La Alhambra that you really should visit. On the slopes of the hill facing La Alhambra is the picturesque old Moorish quarter of Albaicín, a labyrinth of steep, narrow streets and small squares that has changed little with time. To the east

rises the hill of Sacramonte, formerly the home of cave-dwelling gypsies.

www.turismodegranada.es

✚ 24J ✉ 129km (80 miles) northeast of Málaga 🍽 Variety of bars and restaurants (€–€€€) 🚌 Estación de Autobuses, Carretera de Jaén s/n ☎ 958 18 54 80/98 🚉 Estación de FFCC, Avenida de Andalucía s/n ☎ 958 20 40 00 ❓ Día de la Toma (1, 2 Jan); Semana Santa (Easter); Corpus Christi, International Music and Dance Festival (end Jun, early Jul); Romería (29 Sep); International Jazz Festival (Nov)

ℹ Corral del Carbón, Plaza de Mariana Pineda, 10 Bajo ☎ 958 24 71 28

Capilla Real

The Royal Chapel, sanctioned by the Catholic Monarchs for their
burial, was begun in 1506 and completed under the reign of
Hapsburg Emperor Charles V in 1521. It has a richly adorned
interior. In the chancel, closed by a screen, are the mausoleums
of King Ferdinand and Queen Isabella, along with their daughter
Juana la Loca and her husband Philip the Fair. A museum reached
through the north arm of the transept displays items of historical
interest and a fine collection of paintings and sculpture.

✉ Oficios 3 (Cathedral) ☎ 958 22 92 39 🕐 Apr–Oct Mon–Sat 10:30–1, 4–7,
Sun 11–1, 4–7 ✋ Inexpensive 🚉 RENFE station Granada

Casa Manuel de Falla

Manuel de Falla (1876–1946) was born in Cádiz and taught by Pedrell, the founder of Spain's modern national school of composition. He spent several years in Paris, but drew on his own native musical traditions in works such as the popular ballet music *The Three-Cornered Hat*. The composer lived in this house for a number of years. Items on display relate to his life.

✉ Antequerela Alta 11 ☎ 958 22 83 18 ⏰ Tue–Sat 10–1:30
🖐 Inexpensive

Catedral

The cathedral was begun in 1528 on the orders of the Catholic Monarchs. Construction was under the great master Diego de Siloé, and continued after his death in 1528. It features a magnificent Capilla Real (Royal Chapel) and has a notable rotunda, with some fine paintings by Alonso Cano, a native of Granada.

✉ Gran Vía 5 ☎ 958 22 29 59 ⏰ Mon–Sat 10:30–1:30, 4–7, Sun 4–7
🖐 Inexpensive

Monasterio de la Cartuja

This former Carthusian Monastery, which dates back to the 16th century, has a worthwhile collection of paintings and sculpture.

✉ Paseo de la Cartuja, s/n ☎ 958 16 19 32 ⏰ Mon–Sat 10–1, 4–6:30
🖐 Inexpensive (free Sun)

Museo Arqueológico

The museum is housed in the Casa Castril, an elegant Renaissance palace noted for its delicately carved plateresque doorway. It has a fine collection of ceramics from Roman and Moorish times, in addition to some superb Egyptian vases unearthed in the region.

✉ Carrera del Darro 43 ☎ 958 22 56 40
⏰ Wed–Sat 9–6, Tue 2:30–6, Sun 9–2:30 🖐 Inexpensive; free to EU citizens

NERJA

Nerja lies in a fertile valley of fruit orchards, known mainly for the production of peaches and pomegranates. Its attractive setting amid cliffs overlooking rocky coves has earned its reputation as the jewel of the eastern Costa del Sol. Its name is derived from the old Moorish word *naricha,* meaning 'rich in water'. The town began as a Moorish farming estate during the 10th century, a centre of the silk and sugar industries. All reminders of its Moorish past and much of Nerja were destroyed in the 1884 earthquake.

Nerja's promenade received its name when King Alfonso XII was touring the area to show sympathy following the earthquake on Christmas Day in 1884. While visiting the town he stood on the promontory, with its magnificent view of the Mediterranean, and declared it the Balcón de Europa (Balcony of Europe).

Nerja stands out as one of the most appealing of the resorts east of Málaga. It retains the charm of its old town with narrow streets, many pedestrian-only, and lined with whitewashed houses adorned with flowers and crammed with restaurants. These streets lead down to the Balcón de Europa. A series of steps will take you down to the Paseo de los Caribineros and a walkway via several coves onto the popular Playa de Burriana.

Although Nerja has grown into a popular resort, it has managed to escape the sort of development found along much of its neighbouring western coastline. Most noticeably it has managed to retain its small-town atmosphere. Now linked to Málaga by the Autovía del Mediterraneo, expansion is inevitably on its way.

Some 4km (2.5 miles) east of Nerja lies Maro. Perched on a clifftop above a small cove, this pretty village offers good views of the coastline. Of particular interest is the attractive little Church of Nuestra Señora de las Maravillas de Maro, and the aqueduct.

www.nerja.org

🚪 22L ✉ 52km (32 miles) east of Málaga 🍴 Wide choice of restaurants and bars (€–€€€) 🚌 Bus connections

ℹ Puerta del Mar 4 ☎ 952 52 15 31

RINCÓN DE LA VICTORIA

Lying some 12km (7.5 miles) east of Málaga, Rincón de la Victoria is a well-established resort. It offers a pleasant new seafront promenade, some modest accommodation, an 18-hole golf course, riding, tennis and boats for hire. The resort has a reputation for good fish restaurants, a speciality being a small sardine-type fish

known as *victorianos,* and *coquinas* (clams). The Wednesday market is always a great event.

➕ 21K ✉ 12km (7.5 miles) east of Málaga

❓ Fiesta de la Virgen del la Candelaria (1–3 Feb); Fiesta de la Virgen del Carmen (16 Jul); Fiesta de Verano (22–25 Aug)

ℹ Granada 2 B ☎ 952 40 77 68

SALOBREÑA

Some 13km (8 miles) east of Almuñécar is the attractive little town of Salobreña, within the stretch of coast now known as the Costa Tropical. It lies a short distance from the sea among fruit orchards and sugarcane plantations.

Salobreña consists of a cluster of whitewashed houses sprawling up the hill, dominated by the old Moorish *alcázar* known as El Capricho. The castle has been well restored and offers magnificent views of the coast, surrounding countryside and the beautiful peaks of the Sierra Nevada. Also worth a visit is the 16th-century Church of Nuestra Señora del Rosario, which was built on the site of an old mosque.

Much of Salobreña's charm lies in the fact that it remains relatively unspoiled, with few hotels and restaurants. It provides a good gateway to Granada, however, and can receive quite an influx of visitors, especially at weekends. From here it is only 4km (2.5 miles) farther along the coast to Motril, principally known as a commercial centre for sugarcane. Take a look at the Sanctuary of Our Lady of the Head, which stands atop the hill. Enthusiasts can enjoy the golf course.

✚ 23L ✉ 93km (58 miles) east of Málaga 🍴 Choice of restaurants (€–€€€) 🚌 Bus connections

❓ Semana Santa (Easter): Fiesta de San Juan y San Pedro (end Jul); Fiesta de Nuestra Señora del Rosario (early Oct)

ℹ Plaza de Goya s/n ☎ 958 61 03 14

TORRE DEL MAR

Located in the eastern part of the Costa de Sol, Torre del Mar is the beach resort of Vélez-Málaga (► 182), capital of the Axarquiá region. There are unsubstantiated claims that Torre del Mar once formed part of an ancient Greek settlement known as Mainake, which is believed to have been destroyed by the Carthaginians, prior to the arrival of the Romans. These days the town consists primarily of a long beach lined with a string of high-rise apartment blocks catering mainly for summer visitors.

One of the resort's most pleasant features is the extended esplanade which follows the coast to the Marina of Caleta de Vélez. With more than 200 berths, it presents an attractive scene of boats and yachts, offering sailing and a variety of other water sports. Its lively cafés and restaurants also provide a good place in which to idle the time away. Another bonus is the excellent seafood served here in numerous restaurants and bars.

✚ 21L ✉ 30km (18.5 miles) east of Málaga ❚❚ Choice of restaurants and bars (€–€€€) 🚌 Bus connections ❓ Fiestas at Vélez-Málaga
ℹ️ Avenida de Andalucía 52 ☎ 952 54 11 04

TORROX COSTA

Along the eastern end of the Costa del Sol, situated between Torre del Mar and Nerja, is the resort of Torrox Costa. Torrox consists basically of a long stretch of beach, backed with modern apartment blocks sympathetically designed to reflect Moorish architecture.

The resort has been developed primarily for summer visitors. The beach offers a number of water sports, while an extended promenade along the seafront has a reasonable choice of restaurants, bars and shops.

You might like to take a look at the Church of La Encarnación and the Hermitage of Nuestra Señora de las Nieves, both of which still retain traces of Moorish influences.

Scattered along the coast are a few old watchtowers and small fortresses, going back to the times when there was a threat of pirate invasion. Some 4km (2.5 miles) inland lies the old town of Torrox; built up the steep slopes of the hill, its whitewashed houses line narrow cobbled streets.

➕ 22L ✉ 47km (29 miles) east of Málaga 🍴 Choice of restaurants and bars (€–€€€) 🚌 Bus connections ❓ Carnival (pre-Lent); La Cruz de Mayo (2 May); Fiesta de San Juan (23–24 Jun); Fiesta de la Virgen de la Nieves (5 Aug); local fair (4–7 Oct)

ℹ Centro Internacional, bloque 79 ☎ 952 53 02 25

VÉLEZ-MÁLAGA

The small town of Vélez-Málaga lies 5km (3 miles) inland from Torre del Mar, surrounded by subtropical vegetation. Capital of La Axarquiá, it is the centre of an agricultural region known for its production of strawberries and its vineyards, which produce the muscatel grapes from which the famous Málaga wines are made. It is also a centre for the processing of olive oil and sugarcane. Ceramics feature among other industries. If you are here on a Thursday, take time to wander around its weekly market, always an enjoyable experience.

The town is crowned by a well-restored 13th-century Moorish castle. There are good views of the surrounding countryside from up here. The oldest part of the town, known as Arrabal de San Sebastián, is a picturesque area of narrow streets. You will also come across attractive mansions built during the 16th and 17th centuries. Of special note, among the several churches to be found in the town, is the 15th-century Church of Santa María la Mayor, which shows the Mudéjar style. This was the first building to be erected by the Christians following their victory over the Moors here in 1487.

🚩 21K ✉ 34km (21 miles) east of Málaga 🍴 Many restaurants (€–€€€) 🚌 Bus connections
🛈 Avenida de Andalucía 119
☎ 952 54 11 04

ZUHEROS

The white houses of Zuheros cluster below a Moorish castle in the Sierra Subbética mountains, in a world of cliffs and rocky bluffs. A handsome church, the Inglesia de la Virgen de los Remedios, whose tower supplanted an earlier minaret, overlooks the main square, and a village museum displays objects from prehistoric, Roman and Moorish times. The narrow streets of Zuheros make for pleasant wandering, and are punctuated by fine viewpoints such as the Mirador de la Villa. East of the town is the Cueva de los Murcielagos (Cave of the Bats) with prehistoric paintings.

✚ 10D ✉ 60km (37 miles) southeast of Córdoba, entrance to town on the Baena road

ℹ Turismo Zuheros Carretera Zuheros-Baena, s/n ☎ 957 69 47 75

HOTELS

ALMUÑÉCAR
Casablanca (€)
Moorish-style hotel near the centre of town. Spacious rooms with views over the sea or the castle and mountains behind.
✉ Plaza San Cristóbal ☎ 958 63 55 75

GRANADA
Alhambra Palace (€€€)
Old traditional favourite with Moorish-style decor. Close to the Alhambra with views of the Sierra Nevada from some rooms.
✉ Calle Peña Partida 2 ☎ 958 22 14 68; www.h-alhambrapalace.es

NERJA
Balcón de Europa (€€)
A beachfront location right on the Balcón with excellent facilities, including a heated pool, beachside cafeteria, piano bar and parking.
✉ Paseo Balcón de Europa ☎ 952 52 08 00; www.balcondeeuropa.com

Hotel Carabeo (€€)
Near the centre of town and the sea, this British-owned boutique hotel has rooms with sea views, plus a gym and a games room.
✉ Calle Hernando de Carabeo 34 ☎ 952 52 54 44; www.hotelcarabeo.com

RESTAURANTS

ALMUÑÉCAR
Jacquy-Cotobro (€€€)
Excellent French restaurant with beachfront terrace in summer.
Try the *menu de degustación* with three courses plus dessert.
✉ Edificio Río, Playa Cotobro ☎ 958 63 18 02 🕒 Lunch and dinner; closed Mon

FRIGILIANA
Garden Restaurant (€€)
Popular with foreign residents, offering a casual atmosphere and wonderful views. International menu includes Thai curries.
✉ Calle los Cubos ☎ 952 53 31 85 🕒 Lunch and dinner; closed Tue

GRANADA
Mirador de Morayma (€€€)

A famous Granada restaurant located on the edge of the Sacromonte area in an old walled mansion with an almost suburban air. Expensive view of the Alhambra, but the food is excellent. Reservations advised.

✉ Pianista Gracia Carillo 2 ☎ 952 22 82 90 🕐 Lunch and dinner; closed Sun

NERJA
Casa Luque (€€)
See page 58.

Scarletta's (€€–€€€)

Trendy restaurant with innovative menu and stylish interior. There are two outside terraces. Menu includes a delicious *gambas pil-pil* (prawns fried in garlic).

✉ Calle Cristo 38 ☎ 952 52 00 11

SALOBREÑA
El Peñon (€€)

Stunning setting on the rocks with a good menu of predominantly seafood dishes, including fresh prawns with avocado.

✉ Playa de Peñon ☎ 958 61 05 38 🕐 Lunch and dinner

SHOPPING

FRIGILIANA
Vinos El Lagar

One of several shops where you can buy the local wine. Offers free tastings and sells some deli products.

✉ Calle Real ☎ 952 53 40 39

GRANADA
Gonzálo Reyes Muñoz

Fascinating antiques shop with a strong Spanish element.

✉ Calle Mesones (Placeta de Cauchiles 1) ☎ 958 52 32 74

NERJA
La Mimosa
Decorative items for the home, including the work of local sculptor David Marshall.

✉ Calle Pintada 29 ☎ 952 52 02 35

TORRE DEL MAR
Singh
Elegant boutique for women's and men's clothes. Top fashion names, with the latest designs.

✉ Calle Avenida de Andalucía 121 ☎ 952 54 10 91

SPORT

GRANADA
Rustic Blue
For a riding holiday in one of Spain's most beautiful and unspoiled regions, the Alpujarras.

✉ Barrio la Ermita, Bubión ☎ 952 76 33 81; www.rusticblue.com

RONDA
Pangea Active Nature
Offers a range of activities, including caving, abseiling and hiking.

✉ Calle Dolores Ibarruri 4 ☎ 952 87 34 96; www.pangeacentral.com

SKIING
The Sierra Nevada is the most southerly ski resort in Europe and one of the highest, which gives it a long season (sometimes well into May). Its proximity to the coast means you can swim in the sea and ski on snowy slopes on the same day!

Sol y Nieve (Sun and Snow)
This ski resort offers good facilities, with ski-lifts and chair-lifts, a tourist complex and all kinds of skiing.

✉ 25km (15.5 miles) from Granada and 100km (62 miles) from the coast
🕐 Dec–Apr

Sight Locator Index

This index relates to the maps on the covers. We have given map references to the main sights of interest in the book. Grid references in italics indicate sights featured on the town plans. Some sights within towns may not be plotted on the maps.

Index

Acknowledgements

The Automobile Association would like to thank the following photographers, companies and picture libraries for their assistance in the preparation of this book.

Abbreviations for the picture credits are as follows – (t) top; (b) bottom; (c) centre; (l) left; (r) right; (AA) AA World Travel Library.

6/7 Man playing guitar, AA/M Chaplow; **8/9** Alcazar de los Reyes Cristianos in Cordoba, AA/M Chaplow; **10/11t** Man and cart, AA/J Edmanson; **10b** Casares AA/J Tims; **11b** La Giralda in Seville, AA/A Molyneux; **12bl** Tapas, AA/M Chaplow; **12/3b** Seafood vendors, AA/D Robertson; **13t** Paella, AA/P Wilson; **13b** Waiter, AA/C Sawyer; **14b** Tapas, AA/M Chaplow; **14/5** Fresh produce for sale, AA/M Chaplow; **15t** Chef, AA/M Chaplow; **16/7t** Beach bar, AA/J Tims; **16/7b** Ronda, AA/W Voysey; **17tr** Local children, AA/D Robertson, **18b** Bullring in Ronda, AA/P Wilson; **18/9** Flamenco dancer, AA/A Molyneux; **19b** Puerto Banus, AA/M Chaplow; **20/1** Car, AA/C Sawyer; **25** Horse drawn carriage, AA/A Molyneux; **29** Countryside in Jaen, AA/M Chaplow; **28** Donkeys, AA/J Tims; **31** Telephone AA/P Bennett; **34/5** La Alhambra in Granada, AA/D Robertson; **36/7** La Alcazaba in Malaga, AA/M Chaplow; **37t** View to La Alcazaba and Castillo de Gibralfaro in Malaga, AA/P Wilson; **38/9t** La Alhambra in Granada, AA/J Edmanson; **38/9b** La Alhambra, AA/J Edmanson; **40/1b** Casares, AA/J Edmanson; **41t** Casares. AA/J Tims; **42/3** Casco Antiguo in Marbella, AA/M Chaplow; **44b** Cuevas de Nerja, AA/M Chaplow; **44/5** Cuevas de Nerja, AA/M Chaplow; **45t** Cuevas de Nerja, AA/M Chaplow; **46** Seville, AA/M Chaplow; **46/7** Seville Cathedral, AA/P Wilson; **47t** La Giralda, AA/P Wilson; **48/9** La Mezquita in Cordoba, AA/M Chaplow; **49t** La Mezquita in Cordoba, AA/M Chaplow; **49b** La Mezquita in Cordoba, AA/D Robertson; **50t** Jugs, AA/W Voysey; **50b** Mijas, AA/J Tims; **50/1** Mijas, AA/J Edmanson; **52t** Puente Nuevo in Ronda, AA/P Wilson; **52/3** Puente Nuevo in Ronda, AA/P Wilson; **54t** Marina at Puerto Banus, AA/J Edmanson; **54/5** Puerto Banus, AA/J Tims; **55t** Puerto Banus, AA/M Chaplow; **56/7** Flamenco show, AA/M Jourdan; **58/9** Restaurant; AA/D Robertson; **60/1** Golfers, AA/M Chaplow; **62/3** Church in Benalmadena, AA/W Voysey; **64/5** Parque Nacional Coto de Donana, AA/J Edmanson; **66/7** Torremolinos, AA/J Tims; **68** Father and son feed the birds, AA/A Molyneux; **70/1** Paseo del Parque in Malaga, AA/M Chaplow; **72/3** Zahara de la Sierra, AA/M Chaplow; **74/5** Puerto Banus, AA/J Edmanson; **76/7** Spices for sale, AA/J Tims; **78/9** Flamenco show, AA/M Jourdan; **80/1** Museo de Artes in Malaga, AA/J Poulsen; **83** Central Stadium in Malaga, AA/J Tims; **84/5** La Alcazaba, AA/P Wilson; **85** Castillo de Gibralfaro, AA/J Tims; **86/7** Plaza de la Constitucion, Malaga, AA/M Chaplow; **87** Plaza de la Merced in Malaga, AA/M Chaplow; **88** Malaga Cathedral, AA/J Tims; **89** Malaga Cathedral, AA/J Tims; **90/1** Malaga, AA/P Wilson; **92/3** Paseo del Parque, AA/M Chaplow; **94** Fish, Photodisc; **94/5** Façade in Malaga, AA/J Tims; **96** Hibiscus flower, AA/M Chaplow; **102** Antequera, AA/J Poulsen; **104** Antequera AA/J Tims; **106/7** Antequera AA/J Tims; **108** Benalmadena, AA/J Tims; **109** Benalmadena, AA/J Tims; **110/11** Alcazar de Los Reyes Cristianos, AA/M Chaplow; **112/3** La Mezquita in Cordoba, AA/M Chaplow; **113** Coach driver in Cordoba, AA/D Robertson; **114/5** Estepona, AA/J Tims, **115** Plaza de la Constitucion in Fuengirola, AA/J Tims; **116/7** Guacin, AA/J Poulsen; **118** La Linea, AA/P Wilson; **119** La Linea, AA/P Wilson; **120** Marbella, AA/J Tims; **120/1** Beach in Marbella, AA/M Chaplow; **122/3** Beach in Marbella, AA/J Tims; **123** Marbella, AA/J Poulsen; **124** Bullring, AA/P Wilson; **124/5** Ronda, AA/J Edmanson; **126/7** Ronda, AA/M Chaplow; **128/9** San Roque, AA/J Tims; **129** San Pedro de Alcantara, AA/J Tims; **131** Estepona, AA/J Tims; **132/3** Seville, AA/D Robertson; **133** Shopkeeper, AA/A Molyneux; **134/5** Reales Alcazares, AA/A Molyneux; **136/7** Tarifa, AA/J Edmanson; **138/39** El Toreal National Park, AA/M Chaplow; **139** Antequera, AA/J Tims; **141** Torremolinos, AA/J Edmanson; **142t** Tourists in Torremolinos, AA/M Chaplow; **142b** Golf course in Torremolinos, AA/M Chaplow; **167** Frigiliana, AA/J Tims; **168** Almunecar, AA/J Tims; **169** Competa, AA/J Poulsen; **170/1** Frigiliana, AA/J Tims; **171** Sign in Frigiliana, AA/J Tims; **172/3** Granada, AA/J Edmanson; **174/5** Capilla Real, AA/D Robertson; **175** Granada, AA/M Chaplow; **177** Nerja, AA/J Tims; **178** Shrine at Rincon de la Victoria, AA/J Tims; **178/9** Salobrena, AA/J Tims; **180** Torre del Mar, AA/D Robertson; **181a** Torrox, AA/J Tims; **181b** Torrox, AA/J Tims; **182** Velez-Malaga, AA/J Tims; **182/3** Velez-Malaga AA/J Tims.

Every effort has been made to trace the copyright holders, and we apologise in advance for any accidental errors. We would be happy to apply the corrections in the following edition of this publication.

Dear Reader

Your comments, opinions and recommendations are very important to us. Please help us to improve our travel guides by taking a few minutes to complete this simple questionnaire.

You do not need a stamp (unless posted outside the UK). If you do not want to cut this page from your guide, then photocopy it or write your answers on a plain sheet of paper.

Send to: **The Editor, AA World Travel Guides,**
FREEPOST SCE 4598, Basingstoke RG21 4GY.

Your recommendations...
We always encourage readers' recommendations for restaurants, nightlife or shopping – if your recommendation is used in the next edition of the guide, we will send you a **FREE AA Guide** of your choice from this series. Please state below the establishment name, location and your reasons for recommending it.

_____
_____
_____
_____
_____

Please send me **AA Guide** _____

About this guide...
Which title did you buy?
   AA _____
Where did you buy it? _____
When? <u>m m</u> / <u>y</u> <u>y</u>
Why did you choose this guide? _____
_____
_____
_____
_____

Did this guide meet your expectations?

Exceeded ☐   Met all ☐   Met most ☐   Fell below ☐

Were there any aspects of this guide that you particularly liked? _____
_____
_____
_____

continued on next page...

Is there anything we could have done better? _____
_____
_____
_____

About you...
Name (*Mr/Mrs/Ms*) _____
Address _____
_____
_____ Postcode _____

Daytime tel nos _____
Email _____

Please only give us your mobile phone number or email if you wish to hear from us about
other products and services from the AA and partners by text or mms, or email.

Which age group are you in?
Under 25 ☐   25–34 ☐   35–44 ☐   45–54 ☐   55–64 ☐   65+ ☐

How many trips do you make a year?
Less than one ☐   One ☐   Two ☐   Three or more ☐

Are you an AA member? Yes ☐   No ☐

About your trip...
When did you book? m m / y y   When did you travel? m m / y y

How long did you stay? _____

Was it for business or leisure? _____

Did you buy any other travel guides for your trip? _____

If yes, which ones? _____
_____
_____

Thank you for taking the time to complete this questionnaire. Please send it to us as soon as
possible, and remember, you do not need a stamp (*unless posted outside the UK*).

| AA Travel Insurance call 0800 072 4168 or visit www.theAA.com |